# We Called It War!

The untold story of the combat infantry in Korea

# We Called It War!

The untold story of the combat infantry in Korea

By

## DENZIL  BATSON

LEATHERS
PUBLISHING

A division of Squire Publishers, Inc.
4500 College Blvd.
Leawood, KS 66211
1/888/888-7696

6/07 LAD 5/05 4(1)
4/10 Lad 6/04 3(1)

Revised Edition 2001
Copyright 1999
Printed in the United States

ISBN: 1-890622-68-0

Library of Congress Catalog Card No. 99-71599

A division of Squire Publishers, Inc.
4500 College Blvd.
Leawood, KS 66211
1/888/888-7696

# Acknowledgements

Without the support of my wife Eva, my son Denny and his wife Kathie and my daughter Connie, this story could never have been written. I must also make mention of my three grandchildren: Tonya and her husband Keith Kirchmer, A.J. Batson, Lindy Alice Walton and my two great-grandchildren Adrian Batson and Abigail Kirchmer. To all of them I dedicate this book. All of them are what makes life worth living. They are the reason this country must remain free. At the same time we must never forget that "freedom is not free."

A special thanks to my daughter-in-law, Kathie Batson, for all the work that she did on the original manuscript. And also a thank you to my daughter, Connie Walton, for helping me with corrections on the copy.

I also dedicate this book to the best rifle platoon I could have ever been associated with. What a great group they were. They are the reason I have a story to tell. I salute them all. I couldn't have served my country with a better group.

And to the members of my 2nd Platoon who died in Korea, I can only say, God bless you and God love you and keep you. I will never forget you. You have given your all to America and the cause of freedom.

# Prologue

June 25, 1950, was the day the Korean War broke out. The rain was falling along the 38th Parallel. It was still dark when the North Koreans rolled into South Korea in an onslaught that was clearly aimed on destroying the South Koreans and to unify both Koreas under the rule of the Communists. The dice had been rolled, and it was the beginning of a war that would last for three bloody years. Over 50,000 Americans died, and over 100,000 were wounded before it all came to a halt. It was a war that America didn't want, and it would be a difficult war to fight for the thousands of young Americans who would be thrown into the middle of the fire. I was one of those. My story is not about the politicians and the generals. My story features the dirty, ragged, brave and daring infantryman who lived in the hills and rice paddies of both North and South Korea. My story features the men who fought the Chinese and North Koreans in the trenches with hand grenades and bayonets. They were at the Pusan Perimeter, the Battle for Tajon, and the Inchon Landings and at the Chosen reservoir. We were present at Heartbreak Ridge, Old Baldy Hill, Bloody Ridge, White Horse Mountain, Little Gibraltar Hill, Chinamen's Hat and dozens of others. They called us the "dog face" soldiers. I was proud to be one of them.

# Preface

The following is my personal story of the Korean War and the great rifle platoon that I spent almost a year with from September 1951 until August 1952. This is the story of how it was for me as a rifle platoon sergeant in the hills and rice paddies of South and North Korea. I have made every effort to tell it like it really was for all of us in my 2nd Platoon. I wish I could tell the personal story of each and every one of my platoon troopers. Every one of them was a hero as far as I'm concerned. I'll make mention of all of them before my story is over.

I grew up in southwest Missouri on a dairy farm and attended grade school in the country near where I grew up. I attended high school in the small town of Republic, Missouri. I didn't finish my senior year due to the fact I was the only one at home to carry on the chores and hard work of a dairy farm.

When I was eighteen years old and after my parents had died, we sold our farm and I was on my own. It wasn't long until I joined the army in Kansas City, Missouri, and was shipped to Korea.

Prior to going to Korea for a year, I married Eva Etheridge who would be my wife in a marriage that has lasted 47 years and counting. A son and a daughter were born to us, and later on there were grandkids and great-grandkids.

After Korea I returned to civilian life and spent over 18 years working for the Springfield, Mo. News and Leader. After that I went into construction and spent 25 years in the business before retiring. At the present time we reside in the small town of Republic, Missouri.

But as you will see from my story, Korea changed my life completely. In my wildest dreams I could not know what lay ahead for my 2nd platoon and for me. Here is how it was for all of us in a year I'll never forget.

# TABLE OF CONTENTS

# 3rd Division

It was around November 11, 1950, when the 3rd Infantry Division (my division)) landed on Wonsan, North Korea, and began its first days of combat in the Korean War.

The Chinese had entered the war on the side of the North Koreans and were making every effort to slaughter the 1st Marine Division and the 7th Infantry Division. At the Chosin Reservoir both units were fighting south in an effort to escape the Chinese trap through the port city of Hungnam.

On December 10, 1950, the 3rd Division sent a task force north to Chinhung-Ni to join forces with the Marines. Shortly after this link-up, the 3rd Division assumed the responsibility of defending the Hungnam beachhead while the 7th Division and the Marines out-loaded on ships in the harbor.

On December 24, 1950, the 3rd Division completed the evacuation of X Corps. After they departed, the port facilities were completely destroyed.

A short time later the 3rd Division was put ashore in South Korea and joined the fight North against the Chinese. It was in September 1951 when I joined the 3rd Division at a hill complex near the 38th Parallel. It was called "477-487."

\* \* \* \* \* \* \* \* \* \*

I guess everybody in the world has their heroes, but I'll tell you here and now that my heroes are the great soldiers who fought the Korean War. As I will say more than once in this book, "I was proud to be one of them." Some of the things that I saw some of these men do were almost impossible feats, things that were done out of pure guts and bravery.

The Korean veteran, in my opinion, was as good as any soldier this country ever produced. He was tough as nails and gave out no favors and didn't expect any in return. He went out and fought, shed his blood and died for the cause of Freedom and America.

In the early stages of the war the GIs of the 24th Infantry Division fought to the death time after time in an effort to slow down the North Koran army in their efforts to overrun the South. The unbelievable bravery displayed by the badly battered and outnumbered 24th Infantry Division proved to be the roadblock that gave America the time they needed to get more firepower into Korea and slow down, and even halt, the North Korean onslaught. This proved to be the beginning of the end for the North Koreans.

At the Chosin Reservoir the 1st Marine Division, the 7th Infantry Division and the 3rd Infantry Division, who were badly outnumbered, fought the Chinese to a standstill while all three units could buy enough time to board ships in the harbor at the port city of Hungnam and escape the Chinese trap.

In all these battles the guts and bravery of the Korean veteran were displayed time and time again. Even during the so-called trench warfare on hill after hill at the battlefront, the GIs fought day and night and displayed the same great fighting spirit that was shown in the early part of the war.

Yes, I'll say it again, my heroes are the Korean veterans. I was then and will forever be proud to be one of them. May God bless and keep every one of them. They are a big part of the reason why America is free today. I salute all of them.

## CHAPTER 1

# Enlistment and Basic Training

THIS IS ONE MAN'S STORY about the war in Korea. The things I write about here are based on the facts as best I can remember them. No attempt has been made to make any one event bigger than it really was. Let me make it totally clear that I'm no hero, but I was with a lot of great young soldiers who were. Read on and see how it was for all of us in a war that some people called a Police Action and a war that is called the "Forgotten War,' to this day. Let me say, here and now, that the Korean War will never be forgotten by the men who fought it. Here then is how it was for a kid from south Missouri who enlisted in the Army in search of adventure and found more than he bargained for.

\* \* \* \* \*

It was May 15, 1950, when I decided I would join the U.S. Army. I was a single young man of 20 years old when I became bored with civilian life and decided to make it three years with Uncle Sam. I had just missed World War II, and the draft board had been breathing down my neck for two years, so I decided to make the big jump to the military. Now that the big war was over, I figured this would be a good time to get my time in.

Along with a friend of mine I enlisted in the army for three years in Kansas City, Missouri. In a few short weeks we were headed for Ft. Riley, Kansas, for basic training in a peacetime army that we figured would be a piece of cake. We were in for the shock of our lives!

The recruiting sergeant had made it sound so tempting. To hear him tell it we would spend most of our time strutting around the local towns that bordered each side of Fort Riley in Class-A uniforms. In twenty weeks of basic training I hardly ever saw outside, and the number of times I wore a Class-A uniform was zero except in a big Saturday parade or a company inspection. When that was over, it was back to the kitchen for KP duty for the rest of the weekend.

When the day came to leave home, I told my family good-bye and went downtown to the recruiting office. It was here we signed the papers and took the oath. The very moment that was over, the recruiting people turned into totally different people. Instead of being nice and friendly, they all of a sudden became like biting dogs. From that time on, my life changed completely. I began to learn very quickly what it was going to be like in a peacetime army.

We rode the bus from Kansas City to Fort Riley, Kansas, and when we arrived a big sergeant was waiting for us. For the next two days we were issued all our clothing and getting shots at every turn. Most of the time we were doing all this on the run. After a few days we were assigned to a permanent training company. I went to I-Company, 85th Training Regiment, and 10th Mountain Division. After a few days we got settled into our barracks and began a long twenty weeks of basic training. We started in the month of May and trained through, June, July and August. The temperature hit 105 degrees, and it was a "get in and get with it or get out" attitude by the tough veterans of World War II who were giving us the training.

The first several weeks we spent about all our time in the field or in the classroom. After every long day we would spend half the night scrubbing down the barracks until it satisfied our platoon sergeant. It seemed to me that the more we scrubbed the louder he would scream. Once in a while they would keep us up all night. Then without any sleep it was back to training all the next day. Everything had to be just right in the barracks; that included our clothes, our bunks, our boots and footlockers. If they didn't look right to the platoon sergeant, that meant you were a prime candidate for K.P. the next day and weekend.

We had all been issued M-1 rifles, and they were inspected every day. The first time they inspected mine, I was confident they wouldn't find anything wrong. That weekend I was on K.P. I fully believed we had the meanest platoon sergeant in the regiment. Later on I would find out that they wanted us to believe exactly that.

One afternoon the platoon sergeant took us out on the parade field to work on our marching or dismounted drill. After a while he stopped us and called us to attention. He told us to stand still and not move a muscle. I remember well what he said, "Matter of fact, men, I don't want you to move even if a bug crawls in your ear."

Wouldn't you know it? A honeybee tried to crawl in my ear. It goes without saying that I got myself into two more days on K.P.

I had almost decided the platoon sergeant didn't like me very well. After our basic

*Raw recruit at basic training in Fort Riley, Kansas*

training was over, he walked up to me and said it had been a pleasure to have me in his platoon. He told me I was one of his best soldiers and that I could go a long way in the army. Gosh! This guy wasn't so bad after all. I almost got the "big head" after he told me that.

Frankly, I had no complaints about our training. We spent a lot of time on the firing range with the M-1 riffle, the 30-30 carbine and the 30-caliber machine gun. Also, we fired the bazooka and the B.A.R. All of these weapons we learned to disassemble and assemble until we could do it blindfolded. By the time Basic Training was half over, we had come a long way since we left Kansas City a few weeks earlier. We had even begun to look like real soldiers.

The physical training was tough. We spent long hours on marches where we would walk and run for miles with full battle gear. I would find out later that the physical training

3

would be a plus for me. Another plus was learning to read a map and use a compass. The physical training would be put to the test once we started climbing the hills of Korea.

We had completed almost all of our Basic Training when the word came that the Korean War had started. The U.S. would commit ground troops into the fighting. The South Koreans were in desperate straits and, as usual, the U.S. would come to their aid. When we heard about the war in Korea, the first thing everyone asked was, "Where is Korea?" It wouldn't be long until a lot of us would find out first-hand where the place was. However, before I went, I would spend a few months in Fort Gordon, Georgia, and my next assignment after Basic Training.

I stayed around Fort Riley for a while, and then one day I finally got orders to report to a training company in Fort Gordon, Georgia. It was a surprise to me. I fully expected to go to Korea, but for the time being it didn't happen. I had seen a lot of people volunteer for duty in Korea, and I very much respected that, but I figured if they needed me they would call me. I spent the next few months as Cadre in a training company. Down deep I knew that before long I would be heading to the Far East. Most of my Fort Riley friends had already gone to Korea.

I had been in the army for less than a year when I made staff sergeant. I counted myself lucky; yet at the same time I felt like I had worked hard enough to earn it. A lot of men that I saw in the army just didn't want the responsibility of being anything other than a private. However, in my opinion the privates always carried more of the load than the officers and the sergeants.

I married my high school sweetheart, Eva, while at Fort Gordon. We had known one another for years, and even though I was strongly advised against it because of the war, we went ahead with our wedding. We wouldn't get to be together long until I would get my orders for Korea. It wasn't good news, but I knew it would come sooner or later and it finally did.

After spending a few days on leave with my new bride near Springfield, Missouri, I caught a train to the West Coast and reported to Fort Lawton, Washington. It was here that I did all the necessary processing and got aboard a ship to head out to the Far East and Korea. When I had left home a few days before, the hardest thing I had ever done was tell Eva good-bye. Had I known what lay ahead in the next year it would have been even harder to leave.

I'll never forget the last day I spent with Eva before I went to Korea. A deep dread of what was to come haunted us both, and it showed. It was a quiet, cool evening at her father's farm as we walked hand in hand across the fields and meadows together. From the hillside all around us you could hear the lonely call of the whippoorwill. It would be a long time before I'd hear that call again. It only seemed to add to the deep sorrow and dread of being apart. From that day on for a year, I vowed I'd make it back to her.

It's not easy for the wives of soldiers going into combat. Eva knew what I was getting into when I got to Korea. When the train pulled out of the station in Springfield, Missouri, I don't know who shed the most tears, me or her.

Later on she learned she was pregnant with our first child. As exciting as that was, it also added to the worry that something could happen to me. That alone was a worry she had all the time I was gone. We didn't like thinking about it, but both of us knew that it was highly possible that I could get killed. That is the dark cloud that hangs over the wife of a combat soldier. In the end we had to leave it all in the hands of God. While I was in Korea, Eva spent most of her time writing letters and praying for me every day. She lived with her parents on her father's farm near our home in Republic. She is the one person who kept me going during my bad times which happened all too often.

For an old southern Missouri farm boy, all this activity and seeing the big ships coming and going in the harbor was completely awesome. The Pacific Ocean that I would cross was the biggest pond I had ever seen. The big lakes back home were a drop in the bucket compared to this place. A big Iowa farm boy remarked to me that this pond of water would irrigate a lot of cornfields.

Before long we took on all the troops we could, and one day the big ship, "General Meigs," was towed away from the dock and we were on our way. The further out we got, the rougher the sea became, and it wasn't long until half the men on board were so seasick it was awful. I was one of them, but mine only lasted a day or so. A lot of the troops stayed sick all the way across. For them it was a long ride.

About four days out of Japan we ran into a bad storm, and for all of us it was one exciting time. You can't begin to know how wild the Pacific Ocean can get in a storm unless you are there. The waves were three times higher than the ship, and how it ever stayed afloat is beyond me. When a big wave rolled over the ship, a lot of water would run down the stairs into our compartment in the bottom of the ship. After a while it got about six inches deep in the floor, and mixed with all the vomit from the sick troops it wasn't a beautiful sight. The thought crossed my mind that the Army hadn't told me about things like this when they convinced me to join up and see the world. Some G.I. from Tennessee told me, "If I ever get back to the Smoky Mountains, I'll never even wade across a stream of water again." After several hours of the storm, we finally got through it, and the sea began to settle down. Needless to say, it was a welcome relief.

After fourteen days on the ship we landed in Japan and I got my first look at the "land of the rising sun." Being a farm boy from south Missouri, I thought I had awakened in another world. These people and their ways were strange to me. Being in a country that my brother had fought against in World War II sort of gave me the creeps. Every town we passed through on the train that took us to Camp Drake, Japan, was swarming with people. Any wonder it took so long to beat them in World War II. It didn't look like they had been thinned out very much. After a couple of days at Camp Drake we were on our way to Korea. The fact that we didn't stay in Japan very long was a strong reminder of just how bad they needed us in Korea.

The next day I went up on the deck of the ship to get my first look at the land of Korea. We sailed into the harbor at Pusan and prepared to leave the ship. The sea was pretty rough, and one of the scary things I did was climb down the rope mesh that hung on the side of the ship and drop into the waiting L.S.T. that would transport us to shore. A few troops missed the

L.S.T., and they had to be fished out of the water. Pretty soon we headed for the beach, and shortly the boat bumped against the shore. The front gate splashed down and we walked out onto the ground, where I got my first close-up look at the "land of the morning calm." It was one hill after the other as far as you could see.

I began my first day that would turn out to be very hectic. The first thing all of us noticed about Korea was the terrible stink of the rice paddies. It was so strong it would curl your hair. The Koreans used human waste to fertilize the rice paddies. Most of us made a vow we would never eat rice again. We didn't hang around Pusan long until we were loaded onto a train and headed up north to Inchon and the Capitol City of Seoul.

The sergeant who was in charge of the train informed us in no uncertain terms that we were now in a war zone and that from now on we would find out first-hand that he wasn't just talking. "Don't believe that police action stuff, men, this is a bloody war and people are getting killed every day." The chilling words that he gave out were, "Some of you won't make it out of here." What a pleasant thought, but the truth was, he was right. In just a few weeks several of the men riding on this train would be casualties, and some of them would be in my group.

Before long we passed through Inchon and headed for Seoul. It wouldn't be long until I would find out I was headed for the 3rd Infantry Division. They had their headquarters set up on the north side of Seoul, and it was here that some of us checked in with a master sergeant who would process us into the unit we were going to. I was one of the troopers who would go to "F" Company of the 15th Regiment. When I got to my unit three weeks later they were on the front line, and I would get my first taste of how a real live dog-faced infantryman lived. It wouldn't be as glamorous as they make it sound in the movies.

We spent a couple more weeks around 3rd Division headquarters waiting for the day we would join our unit. I couldn't figure why the delay. It turned out we were given a little training in map reading and how to use a compass. All this made sense to me if someone didn't know how to read a map or use a compass. I had just come from training in the states, and all this was just routine for me. I could do either with ease. As a matter of fact, I could have given our teacher a lesson in both. Frankly, I just wanted to get on up to my company. When I got there, I wondered why I had been in such a hurry.

Several days was spent in the hills around the Capitol City of Seoul, putting in to practice the use of both the map and compass. Actually I had to admit it was all worthwhile, especially to some of the troops who hadn't had the kind of Basic Training that I had back at Fort Riley, Kansas. I could see that a lot of army units back home needed to make some big improvements in their training, as some of the troops had no idea how to take an M-1 rifle apart and put it back together. I hoped that before they went up to the front they would at least learn how to handle an M-1 rifle. I guess all that proved was how desperate the army was for replacements. From that time on for the rest of my time in Korea, I said I would never complain about any sort of training we were put through. Lord knows a lot of these troops needed it, and it really didn't hurt me either.

Little did I realize at this time how really important the training I received at Fort Riley, Kansas, would be. Just the fact that I had learned to read a map would prove to be a valuable thing for me. It is necessary for one reason, and that is to call in artillery fire when needed. As a platoon leader, later on down the road, it was a must. Any doubts I had about the importance of my Basic Training were gone in a short time after I hit Korea. I had already learned how to call in artillery and mortar fire and adjust it onto a target. Was I ever grateful I could do these things because I was put to the test early in my tour. Had I not taken my training seriously I would have been in trouble. All too many times I saw troops come to Korea who knew how to do one thing, and that was to look sharp at all times; yet they hardly knew how to take care of an M-1 rifle. Looking sharp in the mud and slime of Korea went out the window in a hurry.

About thirty of us were in the group that was headed for "F" Company of the 15th Regiment. The day finally came for us to head out to our units. My group loaded on a truck and headed north. We had heard all kinds of stories about "F" Company. At the moment they were at a place called "477-487," and the word was they had been doing some heavy fighting and badly needed some replacements. We would be the ones to fill the holes once we got to where they were. A few of the troops would never make it to the company.

I had never been in a combat zone or even near one, so I was in for the shock of my life. For the time being I was as cocky as a twenty-year-old could be, and I had no doubt I could handle anything that came my way. Was I ever wrong? It wouldn't be long until I would find out what a combat zone was all about and the cocky attitude I had would fade in a hurry. As an old sergeant back at division headquarters had told me a few days ago, "When you get up front, my boy, you stop being a kid and become a man, if you want to live. Sometimes you don't live even when you become a man." I never forgot what he said, and all too many times I saw his words come true.

Hill "477-487" complex was a group of hills that was located slightly northwest of the city of Chorwon. A railroad track ran through the valley in the area, and was probably one of the main reasons why a lot of fighting was going on here. The unit that took these hills would have access to the railroad. At the moment the 15th Regiment held both "477-487." Up in this bunch of hills we would find "F" Company. At the moment they were on "487" in a blocking position, and in addition to having a lot of casualties among the enlisted men, they had also just lost the company commander. After I joined the Company, I would hear first-hand the story about Captain Donald Arthur and the charge he led up "464" that inspired the rest of the Company to finish taking the hill, even after he was badly wounded. For his actions that day he was awarded the "Distinguished Service Cross," the nation's second highest medal.

Along in late evening we reached some small hills that lay at the foot of bigger hills that was apparently where we were headed. Up ahead of us was a long ridgeline that ran at a gradual slope up to the hill where "F" Company was located. What a desolate looking place! You could see shell holes all over the place where mortar and artillery shells had landed during the fight for this place. Over in the distance you could hear mortar and artillery fire screaming through the air and exploding. All of a sudden the cocky confidence I had in myself began to fade. Now we were within artillery range of the Chinese, and that made a man get serious in a hurry. You could get killed around here, and proof of it was all over the place. Over to our right on a ridgeline you could see the dead bodies of some Chinese troops. It was for sure; a big fight had taken place here and from the sound of things the fight was still going on. I began to get the message loud and clear. You could tell real quick this was the real thing, and a little later it would get even more real. This wasn't at all like the combat movies I had seen back home. Around here you could smell the dead bodies and see them close up. It wasn't pretty, and no movie could ever capture the truth of this place.

The soldier who came down the hill to guide us up to where "F" Company was located looked like a walking zombie. His clothes were torn and dirty. He hadn't shaved for a while. His eyes were bloodshot and sort of fixed in a stare that told you what he had been through. He told us to follow him and stay at least five yards apart. So in single file we began our climb to the top of the hill and would shortly join our Company. The first round of my tour in Korea had just began. It wouldn't be but a few days until my clothes would be dirty and torn and my eyes just as bloodshot as the trooper who was leading us up the hill. The looks that he gave us were looks of pity. It told me what we were getting into. I asked him if it was as bad as it looked on the hill. He stared at me for a moment and said one word, "Worse." I got the message.

About half way up "487" I was about to experience my first mortar attack. It would be deadly, and it would scare me to death. We were spread out in single file and making pretty good progress when all hell broke loose. Mortar rounds came hissing in and exploding all over the place. After the first few rounds hit they took out two or three troops, and they began to scream they were hit. The next flurry of rounds got two more men, and that made a total of five men knocked out before we had even reached our company. For the first time I experienced the frustration of being fired on and couldn't shoot back. It was enough to run you nuts.

The soldier who had come to lead us up the hill told

*Loren Renz holding B.A.R. at the front in 1951*

everyone to stay calm and not to panic. I was so scared I couldn't do anything but hug the ground and hope I didn't get hit. The ones who were hit were crying out in pain. It was several minutes before a medic showed up and started taking care of them. It was my first half-hour on the line, and I had already seen five men taken out. How quickly a situation could change, and we hadn't even made it to the top of the hill yet. My stomach was tied in knots, and this would be the first of many times I would experience that feeling before my tour in Korea was over.

It was almost dark when we finally made it to the top of "487" where "F" Company was located. They were spread out down the ridgeline in trenches and bunkers. They were a tired-looking bunch of dog-faced soldiers. You could see the strain of several days' combat in their eyes and in their faces. It hadn't been a picnic on this hill, and it didn't take an expert to see that. I was put in the 2nd Platoon and because I was a staff sergeant I was made assistant platoon sergeant. I felt like a duck out of water, but the platoon sergeant said he would help me along, so I figured I could do the job with his help. The 2nd Platoon wasn't very big, and even with us few replacements we were still a long way under strength. I walked down the trench-line with the platoon sergeant and met all the guys in the platoon. When I shook hands with them, what struck me was the fact they all had the same look on their faces and hardly said a word to me. They all just sit around sort of quiet-like, with nothing to say. Before long we would be in the same mood they were now in. It was only a matter of time. Combat does that to a man.

I spent the first night in a makeshift bunker with Sergeant Isaacson who was the platoon sergeant. We took turns standing guard. Every two hours we would change over. This went on all night. Out to our front I watched a machine gun firing all night. The unit that had taken over to our front was in a dogfight with the Chinese. Artillery and mortar fire was blazing away. Ever once in a while a round would whistle over our way. Along toward morning things began to settle down. Sergeant Isaacson told me the Chinese like to attack at night, and later on I would find out that he knew what he was talking about. When daylight came, they would hide out and wait for darkness to fall before they would attack again. This got them away from our fighter planes, which they feared more than anything else. One thing they had in abundance was manpower. They used it to the fullest advantage, especially at night when they were hard to see.

The first morning here was "C" rations for breakfast. I had to choke mine down. It's hard to swallow cold sausage and gravy. It wouldn't be long though until I could eat cold "C" rations like they were steaks. However, I did switch to beans and franks which was about the favorite of everyone else. When a person got as hungry as we did, we would eat about anything. This was one thing I learned real quickly in Korea. Whatever and whenever we were given something to eat, we didn't say a word, we just ate it. That's what kept us going.

I tried to apply that same attitude about food one day while we were still down at headquarters in Seoul. Another trooper and I were out in the hills with a map and a compass when we came across this small village nestled back in the hills. This old Korean lady came out of one of the straw-roofed houses and offered us a bowl of rice soup. We didn't want to hurt her feelings, so we accepted. We both eat some of the soup and it wasn't bad at all. About halfway through mine I spotted something swimming around. I swear it was a live bug. Needless to say, we didn't finish our soup! We thanked her anyway and left the village. To this day, every time I eat a bowl of soup I think about that.

* * * * *

I would be remiss if I didn't mention the names of several 2nd Platoon members who were here my first day. Most of them would be with the platoon for months. Most of these guys were already veterans, and I had the utmost respect for all of them. Sergeant Isaacson was the platoon sergeant, and then there was Loren Renz, Bennett, Marquies, Manhart, Vercher, Twitty, Gomez, Brandanger, Kelly, Ken Whitteaker, Frazier, and two or three ROK soldiers whose names I could never remember. Later on I would meet Master Sergeant Robert Hunter who was the 1st sergeant, and he would become a great friend to me. Stilmon Hazeltine came over to "F" Company as commander. I personally had all the respect in the world for him. He made the job of company commander look easy, even though I'm sure it wasn't.

The day we were to leave "487" and go into reserve, it started to rain. We pulled out of the trench-line and gathered in a small ravine on the back slope of "487." It was here we waited for hours for the unit that would relieve us. Before they arrived it was getting dark and the rain began to fall even harder. We were all soaking wet, and at this time in October it had begun to get cold. So along with the rain we were miserably cold. Someone built a fire out of old ammo boxes and anything else we could find that would burn to make a little heat. It was hard to get a fire to burn in the rain, but we finally got it going. And then someone threw an ammo box on the fire that had a live round in it. The shells exploded and struck one of our sergeants in the leg. We now had a wounded man to carry down the hill. After awhile our relief unit arrived, and we started down the ridgeline to the trucks that waited on the road a half mile away. Our progress going down the hill turned into a nightmare. The rain kept getting harder, and the ridge we were trying to walk down got so slick and muddy you couldn't stand up. It was so dark you couldn't see where you were going. A lot of men fell and were injured. Somehow everybody kept going. We fell and slid so much a lot of us lost our helmets, and a few men lost their M-1 rifles. The bad thing was, all of us carried hand grenades. That made the whole situation worse.

About halfway down the hill some idiot panicked and yelled, "Grenade." You could hear bodies hitting the ground for a hundred yards. No grenade exploded, so everybody started moving again. If we had been able to locate the "panic head," we would have had an old-fashioned hanging on the spot. It wasn't very pleasant lying on the ground in six inches of mud and water, especially as the result of a false alarm.

I spent most of the time sliding on my backside. I'm sure that was the case with all the others. By the time we reached the trucks we were completely exhausted and miserably wet and cold. When we got on the trucks, we huddled close together trying to stay warm. It kept raining so hard that being close together didn't help much. When the trucks started down the road, the wind only added to the misery. The truck drivers couldn't turn on the lights this close to the frontline. That made me wonder how they could see where they were going. After what seemed like hours, the trucks pulled into a little valley and stopped. It was here we set up "pup-tents" in the driving rain. The longer it took to get the tents up, the more miserable we became. After awhile we got set up and crawled inside, wet clothes and all. It rained about all night. Once I got warm inside the tent, I slept like a baby. The next morning we all spent the day drying out everything as the rain had finally stopped. That same day some troops went back to "487" and recovered a bunch of helmets and M-1 rifles that had been lost when we came off the hill. The most scary thing was all the hand grenades that were recovered had the pin just a whisper from being pulled. If some of them had exploded, it would have been a worse nightmare than what it was. Of all my time in Korea the night we came off "487" had to be one of the worst I had ever put in. The total misery we went through was unbelievable. It would be the first of several miserable days and nights before my time in Korea was over. I made a vow then and there that I would never gripe about anything again if I made it back home to the good old U.S.A. I had already seen enough of Korea to put all future plans on hold.

* * * * *

The first time I ever saw him, he came strutting up to me just after we had assaulted a hill during our training period after "487." He was about six feet tall and probably weighed 170 pounds. His steel helmet hid a partial bald head, but it didn't hide the steel gray eyes and the hawk nose. He was as cocky as a bantam rooster. My first look into those gray eyes told me that this guy wasn't afraid of anything. The bar of a 2nd Lieutenant glittered on the collar of his field jacket. Around his waist was a cartridge belt, and hooked onto it was a pearl-handled 38 pistol. This guy was all business, and he bluntly let me know he was the new platoon leader of the 2nd Platoon. After asking me a dozen questions and telling me some of the things he expected from the platoon, he shook my hand and walked away. I had just met Lieutenant Ralph Robertson.

I would find out in the days to come that he was every bit the fine officer he appeared to be. He would be with the 2nd Platoon for a little over two months, and during that time I would learn a lot from him. He was easily the best officer I saw while I was in Korea. During the battle around "487," he had been wounded in the foot and ankle. He had been called on to take a hill no one else could take, and he took it with a unit of ROK soldiers but got hit in the process. It was said when he left Korea he had six purple hearts. I didn't doubt it for one minute. In all the time I spent with him I never saw him get careless or let down his guard. He always preached to me to be sure the men always had plenty of ammo and hand grenades. His philosophy was that you never knew when the enemy would strike. He didn't intend to get caught unprepared.

When he left a couple of months later, I found myself doing some of the things that he always did. One thing that I couldn't do was be half the soldier he was. Frankly, I didn't see very many who could. Most of the officers I saw were not in his league. The army was lucky to have a soldier like him. As for me, it was an adventure to be around him for a short time. I was totally in awe of the way he would look death in the face with complete contempt. I never saw anyone like him.

One day up on the front line Lieutenant Robertson and I were out checking on the troops when we met a major from Battalion who had come down the trench line. We didn't salute him, and he proceeded to chew us out for it. Lieutenant Robertson shot back at him and said, "Major, up here you can get killed while you are trying to salute someone."

The major looked shocked but that was the end of that conversation. Would you believe it? This same major comes back up front in a couple of days and wanted us to escort him to our outpost that was about 200 yards in front of the main line. We didn't ask him why he wanted to go, and he didn't say. So we got our carbines and started out our safe lane to the hill out front. On the way Lieutenant Robertson remarked that we should be aware we could draw mortar fire and we should be ready to get in the first hole we could find. I noticed the major turned a little pale. We didn't stay very long on the hill. When we got back to the CP, he left without another word but still looked a little shaken. After he left, Lieutenant Robertson and I looked at one another and busted out laughing.

\* \* \* \* \*

The last few days of October had arrived and the weather had begun to get cold during the nights. The 2nd Battalion was still living in the "pup tents" and still doing a lot of training in the hills around the company area. We had gotten in a few more replacements and had scattered them out among all three rifle platoons in the company.

By the time the first day of November rolled around, all the new men had been pretty well trained in infantry tactics, and the company was in pretty good shape. The 2nd Platoon had gained a few more people, and we were not too far from full strength but still a little short.

We were soon told that we would return to the front line before long. We would be attached to the 7th Regiment and take up a blocking position behind them over on the Western front. The rest of our 15th Regiment was to go on line near the Imjin River. The Belgian Battalion would fill in with the rest of the 15th Regiment while we were in the blocking position behind the 7th Regiment. All the troops in the 2nd Platoon were feeling pretty good about going into a blocking position. It would be a lot better than the front line even though we would be only abut a mile behind the 7th Regiment and within easy artillery and mortar range of the Chinese. If we had known what lay ahead for us in the next few weeks, we would have been a lot less excited about going into a blocking position or anywhere else.

The next couple of weeks we got a clean set of clothing. The shower trucks came up to the area, and we got a good shower for the first time in weeks. It felt great to get clean again. However, it would be a long time before we would take another shower or wear clean clothes. We were also issued sleeping bags that we could roll up real tight and carry on our backs. Other than that, all we carried was ammo, grenades and weapons.

A night or so before we left this area, we got a big fire going in the middle of the company area and everyone gathered around to soak up the heat. Several card games were going in the light of the fire. I took the opportunity to write a letter to my wife back at home. As we were leaving, I figured I'd better write as we might be going somewhere I wouldn't have the chance for a long time.


*Dearest Sweetheart,*

*It looks like we will be trading our "pup tents" for a hole in the ground somewhere over on the Western front. We are supposed to be going into what is called a blocking position behind the 7th Regiment. When we get there, I'll do my best to write you again. Don't worry if you don't hear from me for a few days. I think of you all the time. I live for the day I see you again.*

*With love,*
*Your husband*

It was around the 15th of November when we got the word to get ready to move out. We were all waiting at the side of the road when the trucks arrived. It was early morning and cold and rainy. Once we got loaded, the trucks pulled out on the road and we were on our way. The road that we traveled took us across a little valley where you could see several trucks and tanks in the ditch that had been knocked out in an earlier battle. When I first got to Korea, knocked-out trucks, tanks and other vehicles seemed to be on every road we traveled.

The small villages we passed were almost totally destroyed. The Korean civilians who were still in these villages were a pitiful looking bunch. I wondered how in the world they ever survived. Some of the small children had no clothes on at all, and the weather was cold. How in the world would they ever get through the coming winter? Korea was a devastated place, and the people here were in a struggle to stay alive. A lot of them would die this winter, especially the old people and small children. At this point in time the war wasn't even half over, and that meant even more suffering for the civilian population.

Good clean pure water was a hard thing to find in Korea. Everything was polluted and unsafe to drink. So most of us got water from a "lister bag." This was where every company stored fresh water that had been processed by a unit of the army whose job was to do just that. We had all filled our canteens earlier that morning, but we were trying to conserve water. When the truck convoy pulled over and stopped for a break, several of us in the 2nd Platoon spotted a small stream of water that sort of ran from around a small hill at the side of the road. What a great opportunity to get a good cold drink. The little stream was clear and cold. We all drink our fill. Before we went back to the truck another trooper and me walked around the hill to see where the little stream came from. About thirty yards away and out of sight of the troops was a pair of dead and decayed bodies lying in the stream we had drank from. We just sort of looked at each other shocked. We went back and climbed on the truck and didn't say a word. All we could hear was how great the water tasted that was in the little stream. Three or fours days later when I told a kid in the platoon about the dead bodies in the stream, he stayed mad at me for a week. I don't know what he thought I could do about it; he had already drunk the water.

After a while we pulled off the main road into the hills. That meant we were getting closer to our destination. In a few days we would be in a battle for our very lives. It wouldn't be long until we would be called on to attack "Little Gibraltar Hill."

\* \* \* \* \*

The battle for "477-487" had been a long and costly campaign for the 2nd Battalion. Casualties had been fairly heavy for all the units that had been a part of the fighting. However, when the fighting ended, it was the Chinese who had taken a beating. When I had joined "F" Company after most of the fighting was over, you could tell very quickly who had lost a lot of troops. There were dead Chinese all over the place. They had paid a heavy price for their efforts to hold "477-487."

After the fighting for "477-487" was over and we were in our training period, I heard a lot of stories from the veterans about how the Chinese would attack a hill with swarms of infantry. Any doubt that I had about the stories I heard would soon be put to rest when I would see first-hand how they would attack in droves on Little Gibraltar Hill. When it was over, the 2nd Battalion would once again need replacements. The Chinese would fade into the hills and lick their wounds. Once again we would kick their rears! The blocking position we were headed for wouldn't last long. But, for the 2nd Platoon, and me it would turn into a nightmare. Little did we realize at this moment the utter hell that lay just a few days ahead.

*2nd Platoon taking a break. In the background is hill "230" where we jumped off to take "Little Gibraltar Hill."*

*Hill 317 held by the Chinese*

*Left to right: Raymond Anderson, James Twitty, Denzil Batson, William Rice, 42 years after the war.*

# CHAPTER 2

# Battle for Little Gibraltar Hill

CONTRARY TO WHAT a lot of writers and historians might say, "Little Gibraltar Hill" was one of the most important hills to be fought over on the Western front. The reason was simple; it was the most commanding piece of real estate in the area. If, in fact, the Chinese could take and hold this hill mass, they could have seen for miles in every direction and could have seen every move that every American unit made. That would have been a great advantage to them. Thus the importance of keeping it in American hands. Shortly after we arrived in the area, the Chinese took the hill, and my 2nd Battalion was called on to take it back. My company, "F" Company of the 15th Regiment, was the assault company. Read on to see how it all started and who came out the winner.

It was sometime around the 17th or 18th day of November in 1951, when my 2nd Battalion, 15th Infantry, 3rd Division, de-trucked on the road behind some low-lying hills that we were to occupy about a mile behind the main line of resistance, (ML.R) on Korea's Western front. The 2nd Battalion was to dig in on these small hills and form a line of three companies that was called a blocking position behind the 7th Infantry Regiment, 3rd Division, who were on the main line of resistance to our front. We were attached to the 7th Regiment at this time because of considerable enemy activity in this area. Our presence here had freed up a British unit to be committed somewhere else on the line in another area. Our own 15th Infantry Regiment was already on line over to the east near the Imjin River. The Belgian Battalion was filling in with the rest of the 15th Regiment while we were in this blocking position.

Prior to us coming into this area, we had been involved in

some intensive training behind the line. Before that, we had been in several days of combat on hills "477-487," over to the east of where we were now. During that period of time the 2nd Battalion had sustained a lot of casualties. When we come off the line, we had taken in several replacements. The training that we had been going through was mostly to acquaint the new replacements with the Infantry tactics used in Korea. Personally, I was a firm believer in the training we went through, and I learned a lot from the veterans who had been here for several months. I had joined "F" Company in the late stages of the "477-487" operation a month or so ago. I wasn't exactly an old veteran at this time, but I had seen enough of "477-487" to realize for sure that this was serious business. I welcomed any kind of advice that would help me stay alive another day. During my time in Korea I saw many young kids who wouldn't listen to anyone, and they usually paid for it with their lives. You only made so many careless mistakes, and sooner or later you would make your last.

The 2nd Platoon was sort of a mixed group, as was the case with all units in Korea. All in all we numbered about 30 people, which meant we were a little short of being a full strength platoon. We had several veterans who had already been here for several months, and about every platoon in Korea had at least three or four R.O.K. soldiers in the ranks. Among the group, of course, were the young replacements that had just arrived a few weeks before. You could spot them a mile away because they had almost new uniforms that made some of our clothes look like rags. You didn't get to change your clothes very often on the front lines in Korea, and as a result it didn't take long until our uniforms would be so dirty they would stand up by themselves. Most of the young kids were cocky as they could be, and they never stopped talking. You could hear some big combat stories from these guys, and you didn't even have to ask them. They reminded me of myself when I first come to Korea. All of that was due to change shortly. One thing I learned real quickly — don't talk too much or some company commander might hear you and let you prove how good you really are. All too soon we would find out.

Our company commander was Stilman Hazeltine, a 1st

*On the left, Sergeant Elmer Brandanger killed in the battle for Little Gibraltar Hill. Center, Master Sergeant Denzil Batson. Right is an R.O.K. soldier named Tom who was wounded in the battle for Little Gibraltar Hill.*

Lieutenant who was a former ranger and airborne trooper. He was one cool customer and the best company commander I ever saw. Our platoon leader was Ralph Robertson, a 2nd Lieutenant who had come up through the enlisted ranks. Robertson was one tough cookie who wasn't afraid of anything. The platoon sergeant was Clayton Isaacson. I was the assistant platoon sergeant. Some of the others in the Platoon were Loren Renz, Marvin Bennett, Ken Whitteaker, William Ray, James Twitty, Sergeant Vercher, Corporal Marquis, Ronald Manhart, Sergeant Gomez, and Sergeant Brandanger who was my close friend and buddy. There was another guy by the name of Kelly (everyone called him "Combat Kelly") and, of course, a few others that I can't recall their names, but I can well remember their faces. To me, every one of them was a hero. Everyone except the new troops had been on "477-487." So about all the 2nd Platoon was a battle-tested bunch.

Lieutenant Gene Light led the 3rd Platoon, and the lead-scout in the coming attack on Little Gibraltar was William H.

Drummond. Lieutenant Pullian and Master Sergeant White led the 1st Platoon. Our 1st Sergeant was Robert O. Hunter who was a good friend of mine, and while in Korea he sort of looked out for me. A few months later I would miss him a lot as he went back to the states.

Some of the troopers in the 4th Platoon were Sergeant Turner, Sergeant Sieber, Sergeant Wimbish and Corporal Tyler. As I have stated before, a lot of the names I have forgotten over the years, but not faces. The 4th Platoon was our mortar platoon, and they gave us great support fire when we needed it.

As we stood on the road and observed three small hills a short distance away, we were informed this would be our new home for the next several days. Over to our right "E" Company was climbing a hill that someone said was hill "238." None of these hills were very high which was all right with me. It would be a lot easier to lug ammo up these small ridges. Once we found out where each platoon would go, we got ready to move out. The trucks that hauled us up here moved out in a hurry. Being this close to the front line they would attract artillery fire if they were spotted. Any type of vehicle was a prime target for the mortar and artillery. I wasn't exactly thrilled about riding in the back of a truck this close to the line. I'd much rather be on the ground where I could get into a hole just in case.

It was cloudy, cold and getting pretty well along toward late evening when the 2nd Platoon started up the hill that we were to occupy. Somewhere to our front, you could hear a few incoming artillery rounds explode. This was a reminder to everyone that we were now where the game again became serious. Every once in a while, you could hear our own artillery guns boom, and the rounds would whistle over us and land somewhere out to our front. A lot of this was "harassment fire" and was going on most of the time.

After a while everybody reached the top of our hill, and the first order of business was to set up our perimeter defense. Some unit that had been here earlier in the war had dug some pretty good bunkers and fighting holes. A trench had connected some of them. This, of course, was a welcome sight to all of us. It got us out of having to do a lot of digging in ground that

24

was as hard as a rock. In all my time in Korea, I never found a good soft piece of ground to dig a hole. We all had brought along a sleeping bag, which would make getting some sleep a lot easier. Everyone had carried up weapons and ammo, so we were pretty well set for the night. After a while things began to settle down.

There was still a little daylight left in the day, and after we had eaten our "C" rations for chow, I went over to the front slope of our hill where I could get a better view of the hills and rice paddies that lay out to the front of our position. These ridges and rice paddies stretched for a mile and finally gave way to a large craggy, quadruple-shaped hill mass that easily was the largest hill in the area. It was easy to see why either side would want to control this high ground, because once on top you could see for miles in every direction. Later on, this hill mass would be known as "Little Gibraltar Hill." The importance of holding it would soon be the cause for a two-day battle that would cost both sides dearly in casualties. At this time we didn't know we would be squarely in the middle of the coming struggle. For the time being our 7th Regiment held this hill, but that would change before long. Our 2nd Battalion would be called on to get it back. It would be a long and brutal battle for the new men in the company. It would be a wake-up call for all of us. After the battle for Little Gibraltar, a lot of young kids wouldn't be young any longer. They would get older in a matter of a few hours.

Soon darkness began to fall across the hills. Lieutenant Robertson and I made a last check on the entire platoon. The ammunition and hand grenades had been distributed to everyone, so we were all set in case of trouble. The platoon was put on 50 percent alert, which meant that one man in each hole would stay awake while the other slept. During the night Lieutenant Robertson would send either Isaacson or me around the perimeter to make sure somebody stayed awake in each hole. Even in a blocking position, in Korea, you could get tested by small groups of North Korean infiltrators. Another reason was, if the Chinese broke through the 7th Regiment, we would all of a sudden "be" the front line — and all too soon, that would be the case.

**********

The night pretty much went by without anything happening. You could hear the usual exchange of artillery fire and now and then a burst of small arms fire somewhere to our front. Every once in a while a flare would light up the area around Little Gibraltar Hill. Even this was a routine happening most of the time. It had been cloudy since we arrived, but all of a sudden the moon broke through the clouds and really lit up the area. You could see shadows all over the rice paddies at the foot of our hill. Every bush and tree looked as if it was walking around in the moonlight. It was a spooky night, to say the least. About then some guy in the 4th Platoon cut loose with a carbine, and for a moment he had his own war going on. It turned out that the trees and bushes had done some walking in his area, too. It goes without saying that a lot of the troops woke up early this night. Before most of them went back to sleep, they pretty much let everyone know what they thought of the trooper who fired the carbine.

In about 20 minutes this same guy cut loose again with the carbine. This time Lieutenant Robertson sent me down in the area where he was to see what was going on and to find out what he was shooting at. I wasn't exactly thrilled about going near him in the dark as jumpy as he was, and I told Lieutenant Robertson just that. Robertson smiled and told me I might "get a Purple Heart." I really didn't think it was a joke, but I went anyway. I didn't trust some "nut" who was as wild as this guy was. When I finally got to his fighting hole, I found that he was still shooting the daylights out of some small trees out to the front. Later someone apparently took over standing watch for him because he didn't fire the carbine any more that night. I told Lieutenant Robertson I would take a court martial before I'd go down to his hole again. Robertson got a big laugh out of that. After I thought about it for awhile, I felt sorry for the guy. Some guys just couldn't stand the strain of being on the front line in Korea — this trooper was one of them. That's what made it so dangerous, walking around in the dark in another platoon area with some nut shooting everything that moved.

**********

The next morning we were informed that our cooks would bring hot chow up behind the hill where we had gotten off the trucks the day before. This was welcome news! Each platoon sent one squad at a time down the hill to eat. This went on until all the company had been fed. The reason for sending only a few men at one time to the chow area guarded against getting a large group together that could create a situation where a few well-placed mortar rounds could really take its toll in casualties. This day the policy paid off. About the time everyone had finished eating and started to climb back up the hill, three or four mortar rounds slammed onto the road and exploded in a cloud of dust. We were lucky this time. When the rounds came in, about everybody had left the area. Nobody got hit — but it didn't take long for everyone to hustle back to the top of the hill. The mortar fire was a strong reminder that it wasn't totally safe in this blocking position. Also, it sent a message to us that the Chinese knew we were here. They never missed a chance to throw in the mortar fire while we tried to eat chow.

The next couple of days went pretty much the same. Everything had become routine. We would go down the hill twice a day for chow, and the rest of the day we would spend mostly loafing around doing nothing. We did keep our weapons clean and in good working condition —just in case. This would take a little time and then most of us would write letters home which would help pass the time away. One day we sent Sergeant Gomez' squad out on patrol looking for "would-be" snipers firing at some of our vehicles along the road behind us. Nothing happened, and the patrol would come back before dark with no contact. Personally, I thought it was a waste of time, but after the patrol went out, the firing at our vehicles stopped for a while. I learned my first lesson in combat. It's always better to do something than to do nothing in a combat zone. By sending out a patrol we had let them know that we could, and would, come after them if we had to.

A few days before Thanksgiving Day, Lieutenant Robertson, who had been in Korea for several months, went to Japan on "R and R." That left Sergeant Isaacson and myself in charge of the 2nd Platoon. Isaacson sort of become the platoon leader, and I was the platoon sergeant while Robertson was gone. This meant that we didn't have an officer in the platoon, and before I left Korea, months later, I would learn this would be the case more times than not. We had several veterans in the platoon, and I figured we could pretty well take care of ourselves if the occasion arose. In a few days we would find out, and some of those veterans I spoke about would be wounded or dead.

********

In no way would I want to short change "E" Company or "G" Company along with the Heavy Weapons Company. The "Battle for Little Gibraltar" would be an all-out effort by the entire battalion, and these other companies would play just as big a role as we did in the fight for the hill. I also would hate to think what would have happened without the support of the artillery or anyone else who helped out. Our mortar and artillery fire took a heavy toll of Chinese in the battle for Little Gibraltar Hill. In the end, however, it was the "old dog-face infantry boys" who did the bleeding, the dying, and took the hill.

It had been a while since I had written a letter home, so on the day of the 22nd of November (Thanksgiving Day) I spent most of the day just writing letters. I come from a big family, so I wrote several letters just to pass the time away. That evening I took the letters down to the chow area and sent them back with the cooks to be mailed. I wrote all the folks back home that I was fine and that life here in Korea wasn't all that bad. A week later I would write another letter singing a different tune. Instead of the easy life we were used to having in this blocking position, it would be a nasty two-day fight just to try to stay alive.

After seeing to it that my letters would get mailed and chatting for a while with my old friend Sergeant Bain, the mess sergeant, I climbed back to the top of the hill and joined Sergeant Isaacson and the rest of the platoon. This promised to be just another long boring night. Neither I nor Sergeant Isaacson was sleepy at this time so we both climbed into a small trench on the front side of our hill and spent the next hour or so watching and listening to the goings on out to our front. The usual artillery fire was being exchanged. You could hear our big guns boom, and the shells would whistle over us landing somewhere on the back side of Little Gibraltar Hill. The Chinese would throw in a few rounds, and this would go on for hours. Every once in a while an incoming round would come over our way and explode at the base of our hill. Pretty soon Isaacson got sleepy and climbed into a sleeping bag. I took the first watch because I was still wide awake. Standing alone in the darkness with nothing happening at the moment, my mind drifted back home. I wondered how my family was doing, especially my wife of just a few months. It was times like this when the loneliness would crunch down on you like a ton of bricks.

*Looking down into the valley from the top of Little Gibraltar Hill, you can see the ridgeline Crete, where we spent a lot of time in early 1952.*

Just a few days ago I happened to read a newspaper some kid had got from his parents back home. You couldn't find a single thing about the Korean War, and that led me to believe that not many people in America really worried about us at all. When I got home a year later, I was amazed at how little most Americans knew about the Korean War. The ones who really knew about the war were the mothers and fathers of the young men who were doing the fighting and dying.

As the night dragged on, I decided to check around our perimeter to see how everyone was doing. I found everyone in good shape, so I went back to my previous spot on the front side of the hill. It wasn't long until the weather began to get colder. The wind seemed to pick up and was blowing out of the northwest. It even began to spit a little snow. In the next few days the snow would turn the Korean hills white.

I began to get sleepy, and it was about my turn to hit the sleeping bag. It was pretty quiet around our blocking position, but further out around Little Gibraltar Hill I could hear some small arms fire and artillery getting a little heavier. After a while things sort of got back to normal except for a pack of dogs continuously barking and howling in some village in the hills to the back of us. I woke Sergeant Isaacson to take over the watch. I crawled into my sleeping bag and lay for a few moments mulling over in my mind the happenings of the past few days. It didn't seem that things were going too bad to me, but then at this moment I didn't know what lay ahead. I went to sleep with the sound of artillery booming in the distance.

The next morning when I woke up I went down the hill to the chow area. It was the 23rd day of November, 1951, and seemingly just another cold winter day. I saw Sergeant Isaacson at the chow area, and he told me that after I had went to sleep last night the mortar and artillery fire picked up considerably. Before morning small arms fire could be heard to our front around Little Gibraltar Hill. After talking with Sergeant Isaacson for a while, he headed on back to the top of the hill. It wasn't unusual for sporadic fire fights to break out on the M.L.R., so I sort of dismissed what Isaacson had said as just another small fight that didn't amount to much. After talking with the cooks for a while, I went on back to our positions on top of the hill.

Later on that morning you could still hear the small arms fire and mortar and artillery over across the way around Little Gibraltar Hill. I'm not sure about some of the other troops, but as for me I could feel uneasiness about this day that I could not explain. I'm not very smart, but ever since we had been here, I suspected that before it was over we would be involved in the ruckus that seemed to be taking place out to our front. I guessed right, and later on that evening we would get the word that our stay in this blocking position was over.

**********

A bunch of us went down to chow that evening, and at the moment none of us knew that the Chinese had just pushed the

7th Regiment off Little Gibraltar. It was said that they hit "E" Company of the 7th Regiment with a blistering mortar and artillery barrage and then followed that with swarms of infantry. I had just gone through the chow line and was getting ready to eat some long overdue Thanksgiving dinner when the mortar rounds began to explode all over the place. I forgot all about eating chow and dived behind the nearest rock to try and avoid the flying shrapnel. What a pity, my Thanksgiving dinner lay scattered on the ground where I dropped it. Pretty soon the rounds quit coming in, and it was then that I made my dash back to the top of the hill. Everyone else left the chow area in a hurry. The cooks loaded up all they had brought with them and beat a hasty retreat back to the rear. Our Thanksgiving dinner was postponed again. Matter of fact, it would be two days before I would eat anything again.

When I got back to the top of the hill, you could see that something was up. All the officers in the company had just been together in a conference, and pretty soon Sergeant Isaacson informed us that the Chinese had taken Little Gibraltar and the 2nd Battalion had been ordered to get ready to move out, make contact with the enemy and take it back.

To say this was bad news would be an understatement. The usual talk and chatter that went on around the perimeter turned into complete silence. It was sobering news to say the least, and now the party was over. The easy days of loafing around this blocking position had come to an abrupt end. Now we knew the ball was in our court, and all of us began to get ready to go and face whatever lay ahead in the days to come. What lay ahead would be two days of vicious and bloody fighting. Before it was over, both sides would pay a heavy price.

The next bit of bad news for us in "F" Company was the fact that we would be the lead Company to be followed by "E" Company and then "G" Company. This meant we would assault the hill and be the first to lock horns with the Chinese. The 3rd Platoon of "F" Company would lead out, to be followed by the 1st Platoon, and then the 2nd Platoon would bring up the rear. Our 4th Platoon would follow up and stop somewhere near the objective and support the attack with the mortars. Everybody in the battalion was getting ready to go. It was a hurry-up situation. No one had the time to scout out the terrain between the objective and us, so all we could do was follow the ridges straight across the mile distance to Little Gibraltar. It would be a long and tiresome walk for the rest of the night. Round one was about to begin.

**********

Just before jump-off time I had a chance to look at Little Gibraltar through a pair of field glasses. The side that we would attack the Chinese was at about a 60-degree slope. As it turned out, it was a good move to attack them from the steep side because during our assault of the hill they were firing down a long ridge-line that ran down to the right that they thought we would be coming up. Before the Chinese could recover, our 3rd Platoon was all over them. They were then forced to retreat to Peak III which would later be the objective of the 2nd Platoon where we would spend a long and miserable day. By noon we would be reduced to half our normal size. It would be two days of hell this South Missouri boy would never forget. Words cannot describe how bad it was. In spite of all that, I was anxious to get on with the assault and get it over with.

It was now getting almost dark, and we waited for night to fall completely so we could move out without being observed by the enemy. All the while our artillery had begun to pound the top of Little Gibraltar. You could see the flash of fire from the rounds when they exploded. The Chinese were throwing in some artillery on the ridges that would be our route of approach to our objective. This artillery fire would be trouble for us all the way across and would inflict casualties on the company before the real fight would ever begin.

Pretty soon the waiting was over and we got the word to move out. In single file we moved off the hill into the darkness into whatever awaited us in the hills and ridges. It was getting colder and was spitting snow. The temperature was about 15 degrees, and the wind was blowing out of the northwest. It would take us about all night to get across to Little Gibraltar, and that meant we would assault the hill about daylight.

We hadn't gone very far until we began to get some incoming artillery fire. It didn't take long for us to stop walking on top of the ridges where the incoming fire would land. Instead, we

*Little Gibraltar Hill — the ridgeline in the foreground was our route of approach to attack the hill. November 1951.*

would walk the sides of the hill to get away from the exploding shells. Even doing this, we had some casualties, and they had to be taken care of and sent back to the aid station somewhere in the rear. It was a miserable night because of the cold. As long as we were moving, the cold wind didn't seem to bother us, but when we stopped the sweat that was on us would try to freeze. About this time, I would have given a lot of money for a good overcoat, but none of us had been issued any winter clothing. This seemed to be the case most of the time in Korea, especially the troops who were here in the early stages of the war.

Nobody knew how far past Little Gibraltar the Chinese had come. That meant we could run into them anywhere. Luckily that didn't happen, and our big concern continued to be the harassing artillery fire that seemed to get heavier the closer we got to our objective. Pretty soon the column stopped, and the word came back to us that a bunch of barbed wire had to be removed for us to continue. Once a pair of wire cutters was brought forth, the wire was cleared out of the way and we began to move out again. It was a relief to start walking because of the extreme cold.

The lead scout for "F" Company (William H. Drummond) was sent ahead of the Company several times to check out bunkers that could hide Chinese troops. It must have been a nerve-wracking experience for him. It turned out the Chinese hadn't as yet moved past Little Gibraltar Hill. That was a break for all of us. When we attacked them, they hadn't expected us to hit back so quickly. They were not ready for a counterattack, and it cost them dearly.

**********

It was an exhausted bunch of "F" Company troops that finally reached the foot of Little Gibraltar Hill. We scattered out in some bunkers that had been dug from earlier in the war and waited for the others to catch up with us. We were still receiving some harassing mortar fire when our own artillery really opened up and began to blast the top of the hill. I watched in complete awe at the exploding shells and wondered how anyone could live through a barrage like that. The heavy mortars joined in, and it only increased the noise that was deafening. While this was going on, "F" Company moved out of the bunkers and up the hill a little further and prepared to attack. The 1st and 3rd Platoons would assault the first two peaks on the hill and secure them. Then the 2nd Platoon would move up through them and attack Peak III a hundred yards to the front. We would wait about halfway up the hill until they secured their objective. Once the 2nd Platoon stopped, you could see the 1st and 3rd Platoons fan out across the hill and start to the top. We waited for the big explosion to happen. It wasn't long until it did. From then on it was a bloody and vicious battle.

The official battle report on Little Gibraltar Hill says that the lead scout of the 3rd Platoon (W. H. Drummond) scrambled up to the top of the hill and even took several steps over on the front slope of the hill. Up to that time neither side had fired a shot. When he turned and signaled for the rest of the Platoon to join him, he spotted three or four Chinese emerging from a bunker, and at close range he opened fire on them. When this happened, "all hell broke loose" and the battle was on for Little Gibraltar Hill. One of the first things I saw was Chinese "potato masher" hand grenades flying through the air like a flock of geese. Some of them landed close to us and exploded.

Our artillery had lifted prior to the assault and was landing on the backside of the hill. Halfway down the front slope the 2nd Platoon waited for the word to move up. About this time the small arms fire erupted all over the top of the hill. You could hear the boom of hand grenades, and then the mortar and artillery shells began to explode. It didn't take an expert to tell that the 1st and 3rd Platoons were slugging it out with the Chinese. Pretty soon the wounded began to come by where we waited. It was then that I began to realize what we were in for. Here and now I must praise the medics. What a great job they did under the worst of conditions.

There were so many wounded the medics couldn't take care of them all, so a lot of them were trying to make it back to the aid station on their own. Shrapnel had hit most of them from the exploding mortar and artillery shells. One trooper came by us who had the whole side of his face torn away and you could see his teeth all the way back. He was holding his face together and trying to get to the aid station. Lord, I felt sorry for him. He was a bloody mess and I wondered how he would ever make it. Later on I would learn that he lived. In a few moments some of the 2nd Platoon would be casualties.

The small arms fire and mortar fire seemed to be getting heavier, and about this time a mortar round exploded just a few yards behind me. The force of the blast was so close it knocked me down. I could feel a jerk on my left arm as a piece of shrapnel tore away half of the sleeve of my field jacket. My ears were ringing from the closeness of the blast, and I thought for sure I had been hit. When I rolled over and sat up, I realized how lucky I had been. Outside of a red streak down my arm I didn't even have a scratch. That wasn't the case with a couple of troopers behind me. One of them had been hit in the arm and leg, and the other which was my old friend and buddy, Sergeant Brandanger, still lay on the ground, and one look at him was enough to tell me that he was finished. Blood gushed from a hole in the side of his head where a piece of shrapnel had hit him. The mortar round had almost made a direct hit on him. While our medic worked on the other trooper and sent him back to the aid station, I watched, sick at heart as my old friend died. The last words he uttered were, "Help me." It was just the day before that he and I had talked about all we would do together when we got home. Now, that would never be, and I felt a great loss and an emptiness that I can't describe. That's how it was in Korea. One moment you had a close buddy, the next moment he would be dead.

Some more of the wounded came back down the hill by where we still waited for what seemed like an eternity. A couple of troopers I can especially remember were the Comoza brothers from the state of California, both of them wounded almost at the same time. They would never return to "F" Company. I began to wonder if the other platoons would succeed in taking their objective. If they didn't, we would have to be committed early. All the while the mortar fire kept coming in and exploding ever so close to us. The word finally came for us to move up. This was it — the waiting was over. We moved up to the top of the hill just behind the 3rd Platoon who had secured Peak I. The 1st Platoon had moved to the left about 50 yards and secured Peak II. Peak III was several yards out to the front and a little higher than where we were now. It looked like solid rock and shale. To get there we would have to cross a little valley about a hundred yards wide. The 3rd Platoon was firing into Peak III to discourage any Chinese who would be waiting for us. I kept wondering what the hold-up was. We were all wanting to get on with the attack and let the chips fall where they may.

About that time, four of our fighter planes came in and began to circle the hill. Someone had called in an air strike, which probably meant that a lot of Chinese were on the back slope of the hill. There was a rush to get air panels out that would tell the fighter pilots where we were and where the Chinese were still holding. Once this was done, they circled behind us and started coming in one at a time with machine guns blazing. I would have hated to be on the receiving end of the attack. It seemed like you could reach up and touch them, they came in so low over us. I watched in complete awe at the show that they put on. Pretty soon they made their last run and headed back south. Now, for us the waiting was over and we made our assault across the little valley to Peak III. The air was alive with machine gun fire. I don't know how I ever got up the nerve to run through it. I could hear the whisper of death all the way to Peak III.

Sergeant Isaacson and a few of the men went directly over the top of the peak while some others and me went around to the right. They made it to the top and even advanced a ways down the front slope and took cover behind some rocks in a hail of machine gun and sniper fire. My group ran into small arms fire almost immedi-

*Peak III on top of Little Gibraltar Hill, the most Godforsaken rock pile in Korea, where I spent the worst two days of my life.*

ately, and some kid (I hadn't even learned his name) got hit in the stomach and went down in a heap and began to scream for a medic. Another trooper got hit and went limping back to where the 3rd Platoon was at on Peak I. I made it behind some rocks on Peak III just ahead of a hail of machine gun fire. I could hear the slugs hitting the rocks just in front of me. A few others made it into the cover of rocks, and from where I was I could see some of the 2nd Platoon firing down into the valley below. Directly below us was another little peak that the Chinese were retreating to. All of them didn't make it. Our small arms fire nailed some of them.

It was from this small peak below us that we were getting a lot of small arms fire. Several of the Chinese were heading on down to the valley floor and were being picked off by the 3rd

Platoon and us. Several of their dead was lying around, and before the night was over there would be more. About this time a Chinese soldier jumped up from behind a rock down the slope just a short ways in front of me and sprinted for the valley floor. I was so startled I almost forgot to fire at him. I had about eight rounds left in the magazine of my carbine, and I fired every round at him. I completely missed and he got away. I was disgusted, and the thought crossed my mind that he would probably be back that night in a counter attack. The last I saw of him he was breaking all speed records across the rice paddies in the valley.

**********

Now that we had kicked the Chinese off the hill, I lay and wondered what would be next. For a moment the firing began to lessen, but once they realized they had lost the hill they really began to pour on the mortar and artillery fire. I can't begin to describe the devastating affect of this attack. Our casualties began to mount at an alarming rate. It seemed to me that every time a round exploded someone would yell for a medic. Our own artillery was pounding them in the valley below, and the deafening noise was unbelievable. Both sides had thrown in white phosphorus rounds, and when the white stuff hit the ground it began to burn a cherry red. It made the top of Little Gibraltar Hill look like a red and white hell that defied reality. It was a hell that would last all day and all night. We wondered if it would ever end.

I lay flat on my belly on the ground on Peak III. All we could do was take it and hope a round didn't hit too close. All too often that would happen with deadly effect. Over to my left and sort of behind me, three troopers of the 1st Platoon had taken cover in a hole that had no top. A mortar round came in and exploded in the hole and killed all three men. One of them jumped out of the hole with blood shooting from the top of his head. He died before anyone could get to him. It was a sight I would remember for a lifetime. I shut my eyes and tried to block out the horror of watching him die.

The mortar and artillery fire was so intense it was unbelievable. I was lying among the rocks just below the top of Peak III, and all of a sudden I realized I couldn't be in a worse place.

When mortar and artillery fire comes in on a hill or a ridgeline, it will always land on the front slope or just clear the top of the hill and land on the back slope. The best place to be is squarely on top of the hill. I looked up to the top of Peak II, and I could see a trench that had been dug in the rocks. I made up my mind that that was where I needed to be. I waited for the mortar and artillery fire to decrease, but it never did, so I jumped to my feet and scrambled up to the trench on top. I hit the ground and rolled into the trench face down. At that moment a 120 mm mortar round slammed in and exploded in the exact spot I had just vacated. I closed my eyes and thanked God; He had let me off the hook again.

Pretty soon the artillery fire seemed to decrease some, and that was a welcome relief; however, the small arms fire remained deadly accurate. Every time I tried to raise up and look around, I was greeted with a sniper bullet that would splatter on the rocks ever so close to me. The thought crossed my mind that "pretty soon this guy ain't going to miss." At that moment to my amazement a young trooper from the 1st Platoon ran past me and stood up in plain view on the ridgeline. The sniper that had made life miserable for me all morning killed him with one shot that went squarely through his throat. It happened so quickly, I didn't even have time to yell out a warning to him. Before he died, he spun around and sat down on the ground with the blood spewing out of his neck. Our medic made an attempt to wrap a bandage around his neck but to no avail. What a sad and pitiful sight, and for the first time I began to wonder if I would make it off this hill. For a moment fear and panic came over me and I had to fight it off and try to keep calm. In spite of all that was happening, we stayed put on Peak III. It was tough to do, but we had to hold this peak until help came.

It was along about this time that I really began to pray to God that if he would let me live through this mess, I would do anything for Him the rest of my life. He knew I was a liar, but as it turned out, He let me off the hook anyway. I thought of my old buddy Sergeant Brandanger who died earlier that morning, and a feeling of guilt come over me. I had to ask myself if I was any better than he was. The answer was no.

The young trooper who had gotten hit in the stomach earlier that morning was still lying where he had fallen. From where I was I could see him and hear his groaning with the pain that must, by this time, be terrible. He had become delirious and I could see him spitting up blood. Lord, I felt sorry for him. Pretty soon a couple of guys from the 3rd Platoon dragged him to safety. What a relief to know he would get medical attention. I never did know who the two men were who went out and got him. The young trooper who had been wounded never did come back to the company, and I never knew if he lived or died.

**********

It was about noon and we still held on to Little Gibraltar Hill by our fingernails. The artillery fire had slackened up some but was still coming in pretty steady. The 2nd Platoon and I were still holding on to Peak III. I couldn't help wondering what would happen next. The Lord only knew how many men we had lost. If help didn't come soon, we would be in deep trouble. I looked around and wondered where everyone was. The 2nd Platoon looked like a squad. I was low on ammo, and I'm sure that applied to the others. Worse yet, if the Chinese counter attacked, we would really be hurting. Luckily they didn't hit back until later that evening. By then "E" Company and "G" Company would be in the middle of the fight.

Over to my left and sort of behind me, I could see and hear our company commander, Stilman Hazeltine, directing mortar and artillery fire on the Chinese. At that moment he was trying to get some mortar fire on a Chinese sniper who had already killed two or three of our men. The duel went on for some time, and after a while a mortar round found its mark. The Chinese sniper was finally eliminated. Of course, it wasn't long until one of his comrades took over and the sniper fire continued to be a thorn in the side for us.

The one man who was really responsible for the calling in of our artillery fire during the Battle for "355" was William C. Moore, our radioman. The responsibility fell on him as the result of all other means of communication had been knocked out. Moore stayed with our company commander, and what a job he did calling in artillery fire. The radio he carried on his back had

40

*On the left — S.F.C. Ledger and in the road Master Sergeant Denzil Batson, near 2nd Battalion headquarters, January 1952, near Little Gibraltar Hill.*

a long aerial on it that got shot off at least twice during the battle for the hill. A radioman in any unit in combat is a prime target for enemy snipers. William Moore would later be seriously wounded at the Imjin River and would never return to "F" Company.

Besides the sniper fire, the biggest thorn in our side was the machine gun fire that had earlier sprayed the top of Peak III. They were still blazing away every time they could see someone. I tried in vain to locate the machine gun in the hopes I could do a little sniper work myself. I never could locate him, but I could hear the death song of the slugs hissing through the air just over my head. Later on, this same machine gun would be trouble for "G" Company when they attacked the peak on the front slope of Little Gibraltar Hill. I was lucky they didn't nail me earlier when we assaulted the peak. We were fortunate we had some cover to get into. Some of the men were not as lucky as I was; they had been hit before they reached the rocks on Peak III. Sergeant Isaacson, Loren Renz and some others who had gone over the top of Peak III and down the front slope a ways were catching hell from the same sniper and machine gun. Shortly we would be relieved by "E" Company, and it couldn't come soon enough to suit us.

After awhile "E" Company come up the hill and took over for us. When they had filled in our positions, we were told to go back to the backside of the hill, regroup and return to "E" Company's right flank and help defend the hill the coming night. It was almost as bad leaving Peak III as it was getting there earlier that morning. The Chinese suspected what was going on, so they began to throw in more artillery and mortar fire. Both "E" Company and "F" Company sustained more casualties during the relief. We moved down the backside of the hill all the way to the bunkers and trenches that we had been in earlier that morning. We scattered out as much as possible to prevent more people from becoming casualties. Lord knows we had already lost enough people. Before long we would lose a lot more.

I got into a bunker with three other troopers, and for a while we tried to relax a bit. Nobody had much to say. We had all seen too much this day. No one wanted to talk about it. Pretty soon I began to realize I hadn't seen Sergeant Isaacson since our relief, and I wondered if he had been killed or wounded. Nobody knew how many men we had lost, but it didn't take a genius to see that "F" Company had been reduced to half its normal size.

While sitting in the bunker, I had a short time to reflect on all the day's happenings this far. We had taken Little Gibraltar from the Chinese but at a great cost, and the party was a long ways from over. I felt weary and heartsick from all I had seen and been through. The fear and fatigue that had come over me all too often could be seen in the faces of the others. It had begun to take its toll, and I had begun to wonder how long this hell would last. I looked at my left arm where earlier shrapnel from the mortar round had almost ripped the sleeve from my field jacket. I wondered how in the world that could have happened without taking my arm off. One of the guys in the bunker asked me that; I didn't have any answer to give.

**********

Our period of getting some rest didn't last long. The bunker we were in had a flimsy roof on it that you could see daylight through. A mortar round came in and exploded within three feet of the top of our bunker. It threw dirt all over us, but no one

*Master Sergeant Clayton Isaacson, left, and Master Sergeant Denzil Batson holding carbine, December 1951, at Hill 236 on Korea's western front.*

got hit. In my mind I could see the mortar crew adjusting the sight on the mortar for the kill with the next round. All of a sudden I decided to get out of the bunker. I crawled about 12 yards up a trench that led away from it when the next round came in and exploded. It was a direct hit and looked like it killed all three of the troopers still inside the bunker. I had missed death one more time by a whisker.

The Chinese then began to throw the mortar fire on us at an unbelievable rate. It was a nightmare — the mortar rounds were exploding all over the place. We were ordered out of the bunkers and back to the top of the hill. We quickly made a dash for it. Every few feet we had to hit the ground to get away from the flying shrapnel. Ahead of me I could see some of the 2nd Platoon sprinting up a path that led back to the top of the hill. The mortar fire was awful, but I caught up with them, and about the time I thought we were home free a mortar round shammed in among us and exploded. For the second or third time on this day I came close to being killed or wounded by an exploding shell. When things began to focus again, I was laying face down on the ground. My ears were ringing and I thought, "This is it."

At this moment, lying face down on the ground, the mortar fire became so intense it was unbelievable. The ground shook from the explosions, and the whole area turned into a red-and-white exploding hell that defied all reason. This was the second time this day that the Chinese had unleashed a ferocious mortar attack. As accurate as the fire was, I knew full well they had to have a man hidden behind us who could see every move we made and who could adjust the fire onto us wherever we were. Pretty soon the mortar fire seemed to slacken some and that was a great relief to us.

When I sat up and looked around, I found my nose was bleeding from the concussion of the shells. Near me sprawled out on the ground were Loren Renz and Marvin Bennett; both had been hit in several places. Loren Renz was hit in the leg and back. Marvin Bennett looked so bad I was sure he was dead. The fight was over for them. I didn't have any time to do anything for them, but I did try to send a medic back to where they were. I had to get on up to the top of the hill with the rest of the company. Before I reached the top of the hill three or four more mortar rounds slammed in and exploded. They were so close I could hear the deadly hot shrapnel sing past my head. It got so bad I told the Lord I would probably be seeing Him before long. He let me off the hook once again and I would live to fight another day.

The last 50 yards to the top of the hill I ran past a young soldier lying face down near the path. We had been ordered to get back to the top of the hill as fast as possible, so I stopped and grabbed the young man by the arm and screamed at him, "Come on, son, let's get on up to the top." Then suddenly I realized he was dead. He wouldn't be climbing any more hills. Sick at heart, I scrambled on up to the top of the ridge where the rest of "F" Company was.

**********

What was left of "F" Company made it back to the top of the hill. We spread out down the ridgeline to "E" Company right flank. It was here we would spend a long night and help them all we could. The night before had been long and cold, but it wouldn't be nearly as long and cold as this coming night would be. I looked around at what was left of the 2nd Platoon. At the moment we looked like an over-sized squad we were missing so many people. I couldn't find Sergeant Isaacson anywhere. I never did really find out what happened to him. I would never see him again, and I could only pray that he only got wounded. Marvin Bennett and some others who had been hit pretty hard would never come back to the Company either. Loren Renz and Ken Whitteaker, both wounded, would return to "F" Company later.

It was getting late evening now, and where we were at the moment seemed to be a little quieter than earlier. However, "E" Company that had replaced us on top of the hill was still getting a lot of incoming fire. While we had been at the bottom of the hill taking a pounding, "G" Company had attacked and taken Peak IV on the front slope. Like "E" Company and our company, they had sustained several casualties. So far they were holding, but with darkness approaching I didn't envy their position. Without a doubt when darkness did come the Chinese would counter attack. "E" Company had been re-supplied with ammo and was bracing for the attack that was sure to come. Our artillery had kept up a continuous pounding of the Chinese and was zeroed in on all approaches to the hill. Our mortars were also ready for the coming storm, and we in "F" Company were waiting for the next round to begin.

About dark it began to snow, and the cold wind got colder adding to the misery. I lay on the ground in a place where I had a good view to the front of our position. I shivered from the cold, and we just waited. It began to snow a little harder, and by morning there would be three or four inches on the ground. Out to our front just across a small valley was a long ridgeline that ran from the top of Little Gibraltar to the valley floor, and it was up this ridge that the Chinese were sure to come. We would have to fire across the valley at them, and hopefully we could hurt them enough to give "E" Company a little help.

When I had first come to Korea I had heard a lot of stories about how the Chinese would blow bugles when they were attacking. I had been over on 477-487 a few months ago and I hadn't heard them blow any bugles, but this night I would hear them loud and clear. Apparently, this was the method they used to start an assault and when they had to retreat. Rumors were that they would sometimes play a tune such as "Good Night Irene," or several other American songs that were popular back then. This night they wouldn't play us any tunes, but they did blow the bugles and before it was all over they had been stopped again and again by "E" Company, who in my opinion put up one gallant effort this night. If they hadn't, we would have lost the hill.

(*Author* — Based on information I received from my First Sergeant, Robert O. Hunter, I discovered that Master Sergeant Isaacson did return to "F" Company for a short time after "355" and then rotated home. I apologize for the mistake.)

\*\*\*\*\*\*\*\*\*

It was beginning to get dark and the snow was still falling when the Chinese launched their first counter attack. After a struggle they succeeded in pushing "G" Company off Peak IV. On the front slope of the hill, however, they didn't make it any further up the hill because of the terrific amount of fire that was brought to bear on them. When they hit again, they would come after "E" company in an effort to retake all they had lost to us earlier that morning. They began to throw the mortar and artillery at "E" Company, and our own artillery was pounding the ridgeline that led to the top of the hill. Flares lit up the sky with an eerie looking light, and the white snow on the ground made it look even brighter. The small arms fire had almost stopped which could only mean one thing — they were regrouping for another try at the hill. Just before the next counter attack, a couple of Chinese troops wandered over close to us. I can tell you for sure, they wouldn't be in the next attack. Did I feel bad about that? Not at all. At this stage of the game I didn't feel anything. From the beginning it was kill or be killed.

After a while I heard the eerie blast of a bugle, and the Chinese launched another counterattack. This time they came after "E" Company, hammer and tongs. When it was all over, they were forced to retreat again with considerable losses. I don't know how many, but they had to have been hurt pretty bad. "E" Company didn't budge and prepared for the next round. From where I was on "E" Company's right flank, you could see the Chinese trying to regroup for another try. I lay flat on the ground, and when I could see someone in range I would fire in the hopes of hitting them. I'm not sure if I ever did; in the light of a flare it was hard to tell.

The struggle continued throughout the night, and time after time the Chinese counterattacked. I lost count of how many times they tried to take back the hill. The commander of "E" Company flatly refused to give it up. Time after time they stopped the Chinese cold. Ammunition began to get scarce, and there was a desperate attempt to re-supply them. Ammo that was meant for "G" Company and us was handed over to "E" Company because most of the attack was coming at the high part of the hill where they were holding.

The night dragged on, and a few hours before daylight they hit again. This time they were more fanatical than ever. They succeeded in getting onto Peak III. Again "E" Company rose to the task and after some desperate hand-to-hand fighting stopped them again. Soon the Chinese gave up the effort. They retreated back down the hill under a hail of artillery and mortar fire. I lay in our position and watched in disbelief at the exploding shells that landed among the retreating Chinese. How anyone could have lived through that barrage is beyond me.

The next morning I could see that a lot of the Chinese didn't make it. They didn't counterattack again, and you could sense that the battle for Little Gibraltar was over and we had won! The number of times they counterattacked the hill was proof of how much both sides wanted to win. It was proof of how important the hill was to them and us. For the time being it belonged to us. We paid a heavy price in G.I. blood.

**********

The firing from both sides began to subside, and by mid-morning it had almost ceased altogether. For the first time in a long while I had a chance to see just how many people were left in the 2nd Platoon. I counted 12 or 14, and the other platoons were not much better off. The 2nd Battalion would need some more replacements after this day. Later I would learn that a lot of people had gone back to the rear with frostbitten hands and feet. That accounted for some of the shortage of manpower we experienced that last night on the hill. A lot of these people rejoined the company a few days later. As for me, I was thankful I had made it thus far, and in spite of all that had happened to us, I felt a sense of pride in being here for the last round.

It stopped snowing but was still cold. About this time I realized I hadn't eaten anything for almost two days and hadn't even taken a drink of water. All of us were dead tired and needed to get off the hill and get some sleep and something to eat and drink. If we didn't, I doubt any of us would have made it off the hill at all. We looked and acted like a bunch of zombies. I was so worn out and so fatigued I was seeing double. I had about reached my limit. I hoped that in our condition we wouldn't spend another night on this hill.

Along in the evening, we got the word that the 7th Regiment would relieve us, and we were to get ready to move off the hill as soon as they arrived. What a relief, for as tired as I was I felt like shouting. It was hard to believe that this ordeal was really over for us. We found out that tents had been set up for us a few miles back down the road and that we would have hot chow and coffee when we got there. We eagerly waited for our relief. Pretty soon they came up the road that sort of circled around the backside of Little Gibraltar. This would be the same road that would lead us back to the tents where we were to assemble. When we began to be replaced by the 7th Regiment, we moved down the hill and onto the road in single file. Most of all, I couldn't wait to get something to eat and drink. The 2nd Platoon was bringing up the rear of the column. What a relief to be leaving this place! I fully expected to be hit with artillery fire as we moved down the road, but it didn't happen. We must have really kicked their rear!

As glad as I was that it was over, I felt a deep sadness for the ones who had died on this hill. I thought of my old friend, Sergeant Brandanger, and for a moment the emotion took over. He had been a good friend to me. When I had first come to Korea, he had sort of taken me under his wing and helped me out in a lot of ways. I took a last look up the hill where he had died the morning before; then I moved on down the road with the others.

Just prior to reaching the road, we caught up with some Koreans carrying a wounded GI on a stretcher. Some young lieutenant was just behind the Koreans when all of a sudden they dropped the wounded GI on the ground. He groaned with pain, and you could tell it really hurt him. The lieutenant screamed at the Koreans to pick up the wounded man. "Pick him up, and don't you dare drop him again, and if you do, I'll make you wish you hadn't. Do you understand me?" The Koreans wasted no time in picking up the wounded GI. It was plain they understood the lieutenant. When I walked by them, I'm on the lieutenant's side, so don't drop him again. The lieutenant stayed on their tail until the wounded man was loaded on a jeep. The Koreans were glad to get away from the young officer. If they had dropped the wounded man again, I had no doubt he would carry out his threat. I had never seen him before, but I liked his attitude.

As we walked along the road, I couldn't get my mind off the ones who had died on this hill. It wouldn't be long now until a lot of mothers and fathers back home would get the word that they had lost a son. What a blow it would be for them. I especially felt for the family of my old buddy, Sergeant Brandanger. I never did hear from any of the families, but then I'm not sure they could have ever found me even if they had tried, we were on the move so much.

A little further down the road just before we reached our assembly area, a kid who was a news reporter for some magazine back in the States approached me and asked if it was pretty bad up on the hill? I only glared at him and didn't answer. He quickly turned and walked away to find someone else in a better frame of mind than I was. Later on, after I thought about it, I felt sorry that I had treated him that way. I should have told him it was worse than "hell" on Little Gibraltar hill.

Pretty soon we reached the area where the tents had been set up. Several people were already waiting for us. We were an awful looking bunch of troopers, and some of the people there told us just how bad we really looked! We ignored the remarks, and I for one headed for the chow line in another tent nearby.

I left my carbine and helmet in my sleeping bag. When I approached the chow line, my old friend Sergeant Bain hardly recognized me. He told me that I looked like I had been to hell and back. The thought crossed my mind, "Did I really look that bad?" By the time I had eaten chow and drank all the hot coffee I wanted, it was getting almost dark when I got back to our sleeping tent. I lay down on my sleeping bag, and in the distance I could hear the rumble of artillery fire. For a moment I lay awake, and then complete fatigue took over. I didn't wake up for 10 hours.

**********

When I woke up the next morning, some of the troopers were still sleeping and some were already eating chow. I joined the chow line and made short work of a big breakfast of eggs and bacon and hot coffee. When we went back over to our sleeping tent, I discovered that Lieutenant Robertson had returned from Japan. It took an hour to bring him up to date on all that had happened since he had left the company several days ago. After I had finished talking to him, when he got up to leave he told me I would be his platoon sergeant replacing Sergeant Isaacson. I wasn't sure I wanted the job, but I told him I would do my best. I asked him what had happened to Isaacson. He didn't know for sure. I never found out.

In a few days we got in some new replacements, and along with some returning casualties the 2nd Platoon began to look more like it should. I very much missed the ones who wouldn't be with us anymore. We would stay here a few more days. The rest and the food quickly helped us to get going again. All of us who had made it through the past few days had grown up a lot, and we just didn't have much to say up until now. After a while we began to open up and talk more. It wasn't long until we started to act normal again. One thing that happened to me, after Little Gibraltar hill, I found it hard to smile again.

We all knew our time here was drawing to a close. One night just before we were to leave we all got together in one of the big tents and threw a party. A couple of guys from the 1st Platoon came up with a guitar and mandolin. They played country music and sang songs until late that night. Everybody joined in on each song until the wee hours of the morning.

Finally, the company commander decided the party had gone on long enough and it came to a halt. Everybody hated to see the fun stop, but we were supposed to get ready to move out of here the next day or so, and orders were orders.

Before I turned in for a little sleep, I went outside the tent for a little fresh air. It was a clear cold night and the stars in the sky numbered in the millions. A full moon hung in the sky and lit up the surrounding hills with light. Off in the distance I could hear the boom of artillery fire, which was a grim reminder that the war was still on. I shook off the feelings of loneliness and went inside to get some sleep.

The next evening we were told to get ready to move out. We were heading east to rejoin the 15th Regiment, still on line somewhere near the Imjin River. The next morning the trucks came and we loaded up and headed down the road. I looked back to the north, and I could see Little Gibraltar Hill rising into the sky. I wondered if I would ever see this place again. As we rounded a bend in the road, Little Gibraltar Hill faded in the distance. As for me and the 2nd Platoon, our next encoun-

*The small valley at Peak Three on top of Little Gibraltar Hill where I thought I would surely die.*

ter with the Chinese was coming up north of the Imjin River on a moonlit night a week or so before Christmas, but then, that is another story.

**********

The events and happenings that took place on Little Gibraltar Hill those two long days are branded across my mind and my soul after all these years. If I live to be a hundred years old, I'll never forget the great soldiers of "F" Company who kicked the Chinese off Little Gibraltar Hill or the troops of both "E" and "G" Companies who shared the fighting with us. I would be remiss if I didn't include all the supporting elements such as the artillery and the mortar companies. The medics did a great job under trying conditions, which is always the case in a combat situation.

All the events that I wrote about are the things that happened in my area. Other people who were there could tell a different story than I have because things happened where they were that didn't happen near me. It's for sure the troops of my 2nd Platoon are the ones I was the closest to and the ones I was with on Peak III. My hat is off to them. What a great group they were. We took a terrible pounding while on Peak III, but we did hang on until relief finally came. Later on in the war we would have other fights with the Chinese, but probably none of them were as important as the battle of "Little Gibraltar Hill."

# Korean Peninsula

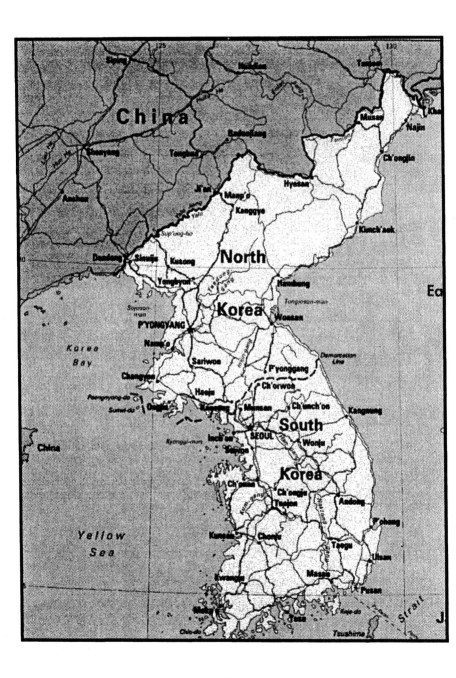

*Lt. Stilman Hazeltine, C.O. of F Co mpany, and Denzil Batson, 41 years after Korea.*

# CHAPTER 3

# O'Conell Pass

AFTER THE BATTLE for Little Gibraltar Hill, the Korean War changed into what was called "trench warfare." Instead of pushing the enemy and taking more ground, it turned into a stationary battle that was going to cost as many casualties. And possibly more than the amount in the first year of the war. Both sides dug in deeper and brought up more fire power. The no-man's land that lay between the two armies would be the stage for deadly firefights that would increase the number of dead and wounded. To all of us troops on the front line it was a constant battle just to try to stay alive, which was nothing new to an infantryman. At night it was especially dangerous because it allowed the enemy to slip into our perimeter under cover of darkness. And if you didn't stay alert you might not see another day. Outpost duty was the most dangerous because the outpost itself was several hundred yards out in front of the M.L.R. That meant that just a handful of men were vulnerable to any larger force that might attack them. A lot of times they would be cut off from the M.L.R. and either be killed or captured. Outpost duty was a dirty, dangerous business and was a dreaded job to any soldier on the front. Patrol action was an every night business for everyone, and not a night passed but what someone would be in a deadly firefight with the enemy. The 2nd Battalion would be involved in several of these skirmishes at our next destination which was along the banks of the Imjin River and was called "O'Connell Pass." As usual, the 2nd Platoon of "F" Company would get its share of the action.

\* \* \* \* \*

It was the 1st day of December 1951 when the 2nd Battalion of the 15th Regiment arrived at its new position, a place called "O'Conell Pass," just south of the Imjin River on Korea's west central front. It had been two weeks since the battalion had battled for Little Gibraltar Hill, and we were getting ready to take over for a unit in this area. When the trucks we were riding in pulled into a semi-circle and stopped, we knew we had arrived at our destination. On the ride over here it had started raining, and all of us were soaking wet and miserably cold. The trucks had no top, so staying dry was impossible. It was a pleasure to get on the ground and move around some to get the blood flowing again. Sometimes I wondered if we ever had a day when it wasn't raining or snowing in this place. The weather was something an infantryman was always concerned about. We lived out in it 24 hours a day. One of the men asked me, "Sarge, has there been one day go by that we haven't been wet as a drowned rat?"

The 2nd Platoon of "F" Company gathered by the side of the road and waited for the word to move out to our new positions. The trucks, as always, moved out in a hurry back to the rear. When they came rolling by us, several of the troopers yelled out and told them to "Stay ready back at battalion. If they overrun us, you guys are next." I'm not sure how the truck drivers took this, but I can tell you for sure none of them smiled at us as they went by. All of us had a big laugh out of this. I'm sure the truck drivers called us a few choice names on down the road. Frankly, we could care less what the people behind us said. It's for sure, none of them ever offered to trade places with us.

Looking up at the surrounding hills, I was amazed at how big they were. From where we stood on the road to the top of these monsters looked like a three-mile walk, and we would be carrying weapons and ammunition all the way. It goes without saying that the troops of my platoon had a few choice words to say about this place and Korea in general. As a matter of fact, I had a few choice words of my own. On the way up the hill I used every one of them. I wondered if we would have to walk the distance twice a day to eat chow. For sure, you couldn't get a vehicle any closer than where we now were. Sometimes I wondered if there was one square inch of Korea that wasn't a hill. Carrying ammo and weapons up these mountains would test the stamina of any man.

Lieutenant Robertson, our platoon leader, came over to us

and informed us it was time to go. Frankly, I was glad to get moving. I wanted to get onto our perimeter defense before dark and also get a look at the surrounding terrain. Getting familiar with our new positions on the front line is something I learned from Lieutenant Robertson. It always paid off. If I were going to take out patrols in this area, I sure didn't want to get lost and walk into the Chinese M.L.R.

We moved in behind the other platoons and started our climb to the top of the hill. It took us 45 minutes or longer to get there, and everyone agreed it seemed like 10 miles instead of one mile. Surprisingly, once we reached the top of the hill it flattened out for about 50 yards before beginning a gradual slope to the rice paddies in the valley floor. We set up our perimeter defense in the middle of the company with the 1st Platoon on our right occupying a ridgeline that pointed toward the Imjin River. To our left the 3rd Platoon occupied another ridgeline that also curved slightly toward the river out to our front. We actually formed a horseshoe-shaped perimeter with us in the backside of the curve. Down to our front and bordered on each side by the ridges were rice paddies that stretched all the way to the Imjin River. The stink from the rice paddies in this area would put a skunk to shame. The river snaked out of the hills from our left and disappeared again into the hills on our right. Across the Imjin River on the Chinese side a sandbar about 50 feet wide extended for a half mile before giving way to a 30-foot bluff that bordered the north side of the river for a considerable distance. On the face of this bluff was a thick growth of grapevines that before long would be my way to escape being killed or taken prisoner by the Chinese. It would be an experience I would never forget.

At the fringe of the sandbar that lay across the river the hills rose abruptly. It was one hill after the other as far as you could see. At the moment a blue haze hung over the hills held by the enemy. It was a beautiful late evening sight, but it didn't keep me from wondering how many thousand enemy soldiers were lurking behind the distant ridges waiting for us to make a move or a mistake so they could hang us out to dry. Likewise, we would take any opportunity to do them the same favor.

**********

*Master Sergeant Denzil Batson standing near 2nd Platoon C.P., December 1951, near the Imjin River.*

Before darkness began to fall across the hills of Korea, the squad leaders, along with Lieutenant Robertson and me, placed all our troopers in bunkers and fighting holes that were already there, compliments of the unit we had just relieved. As always, we made sure everyone had plenty of ammo and grenades. Our machine guns were placed in the best possible position so as to cover as much of the terrain as possible. Our rifleman and BAR people were placed around in the best location, so we felt like we could give anyone a lot of trouble if we were attacked. I told our replacements that this was not a blocking position or a place or a time to relax and "let down your guard." In fact, the only thing between the Chinese and us was a quarter mile of rice paddies and the Imjin River. Of course, the river was the line drawn in the sand, and both sides dared the other to cross it. Would you believe it, the 2nd Platoon would be the first to take the dare.

After I made my little speech to all the new guys, I had the feeling that what I had just said went in one ear and out the other. In a few nights all of us would find out first hand that the hills to our front were crawling with Chinese and they would make a spirited effort to make the 2nd Platoon permanent guests in a North Korean prison.

To me, one of the most frustrating things a platoon sergeant was faced with was to convince new men of the real danger on the front line. Too many times a new man would never learn to be alert until it was too late. It's hard to learn anything when you are dead. Carelessness is the biggest enemy to a front-line soldier. It probably cost us as many casualties as anything else did.

Our first night here settled in clear and cold. The rain had departed and there wasn't a cloud in the sky. A million stars were out, and a bright full moon hung in the sky and lit the area up like it was daylight. I was convinced that this was an ideal night for the Chinese to be on the prowl. Looking across the Imjin, you could see the dark outline of the hills occupied by the enemy. The whole scene looked peaceful, but in spite of all that I was as jumpy as a cat this night. Every time we replaced another unit on the line, I always feared we would be attacked during the changeover. About that time one of my squad leaders whistled over the sound power phone that was hooked up to the Platoon CP and told me he thought he saw movement in the rice paddies to our front. Nothing ever came of it, but everyone on the perimeter could smell Chinese. It was enough to make us all stay wide awake all night. These alerts happened all the time in Korea. You didn't ignore any of them. If you did, it could be a big and costly mistake. You can bet that the company commander had our mortars and the artillery alerted just in case. After awhile it began to get daylight, and about this time with things settled down I crawled inside our CP and got some much-needed sleep.

Early that morning I was jolted awake by exploding mortar rounds. I grabbed my carbine and rushed outside, fully expecting an attack to be coming. It turned out the Chinese were only throwing in harassing fire just to let us know they were around. No one went down the hill for chow until we were sure that no attack was coming. Not many people wanted to venture very far out in the open anyway with the mortar rounds coming in. When the firing stopped, everyone went down to chow in small groups. I was still jumpy as a cat until everyone got back to the perimeter. Lieutenant Robertson told me to head for the chow area and get something to eat. I headed down the hill we had climbed the day before. It wasn't bad going down, but when I finished eating chow and started back to the top I wondered if it was worth it. Once again I vented a few choice words on the hill I was climbing.

**********

The cold days of December passed slowly, and Christmas was just around the corner. Everyone talked of home and family at this time of the year, but all of us knew that all those good things would be just pleasant thoughts this year. Each day that passed would find us out on patrol or just carrying on the routine duties around our perimeter. A few firefights had broken out in the area around us, but so far the Chinese had left us alone. However, most of us figured it would be just a matter of time until they tried us out. What surprised me a few nights later was that "F" Company would be the first to stir up trouble. For me personally it would be a long and exciting night.

It all started when Lieutenant Robertson was called down to Battalion to discuss a platoon-size patrol that would be our first time to cross the Imjin River since we had been here. It was supposed to be an "ambush patrol," which meant we would try to kill Chinese or maybe capture prisoners. The only thing I didn't like about this patrol was how deep we would go into the hills north of the river. I put up a mild protest but to no avail. Tonight it would be 2nd Platoon against the whole Chinese army. I really couldn't see what could be gained by this operation, but you don't argue with your commanding officers — orders are orders. One thing was for sure, the Chinese didn't take kindly to us playing in their front yard, and we were due to find that out — loud and clear.

Along about noon I went down to our perimeter and went over our patrol plans for the coming night with all the squad leaders. One thing that we always planned on patrols, if we got hit hard we always had a pre-planned spot for the platoon to reassemble. Tonight it would be on our side of the river — at

*James Twitty, long-time member of the 2nd Platoon Company "F," at the front line somewhere in Korea.*

the spot where we crossed over. It doesn't make any difference how much planning goes into a combat operation; it always changes once the fight starts. This night would be no different. When things happen you don't count on, you have to adjust to the situation, whatever it is.

After making sure our ammo and hand grenades were in plentiful supply, I started back to the Platoon CP. I was keyed up and ready to go get this patrol over with. One of my troopers in the 1st Squad stopped me and told me with a grin, "Don't look so downhearted, Sarge, maybe they will throw us a Christmas party when we get across the river." I told him I hoped it would be a Christmas party and not a going-away party. It never ceased to amaze me how GI's could have such a great sense of humor in the face of real danger.

*********

Darkness found us moving single file along the rice paddies and toward the Imjin River. At the moment it was a cloudy cold night with a little bit of snow falling. We finally reached the river, and before we started across Lieutenant Robertson reminded everyone that here was where we would assemble in case we got hit hard and had to make a fast retreat back across the river. I didn't say anything, but I would have bet a lot of money that we would be coming back before this night was over, in a hurry. We entered the water and started across. It was as cold as ice, and by the time we had gotten halfway across it came up to our waist. The cold water against your skin made your teeth chatter. I wondered how much deeper it would get, but surprisingly it began to get shallower as we progressed across. About the time we all reached the north side, the moon broke through the clouds and you could see for a mile in every direction. I held my breath. I was sure the Chinese would spot us, but nothing happened. We continued down a wide sandbar that ran along beside the river. After about 300 yards we found a small cut, or ravine, between two small hills, so we started climbing a gradual slope that led to the top of a hill that I swear couldn't have been more than a few hundred feet from the Chinese MLR. It was here that we set up our perimeter defense and the long agonizing wait began. I had the bad feeling that the Chinese had deliberately let us get this close so they could surround us and destroy us. It wouldn't be very long until they were making a spirited effort to do just that.

A half-hour passed. I was as jumpy as a cat. You could smell Chinese all over the place. There wasn't a doubt in anyone's mind that the party would be starting before much longer. The moon broke through the clouds and lit the area up all around us. Down just below where Lieutenant Robertson and I were on the front slope, I spotted movement. A bunch of Chinese was moving around to our left side and the others were coming up the hill straight at us. Before I could let anyone know what I had seen, a "burp gun" barked and the slugs tore through the air like angry bees all around us. Luckily, no one was hit. I pulled the pin on a hand grenade and threw it down the hill. I hoped it would slow them down, but I never knew if it did nor not. However, when the grenade exploded, I heard someone yelp. Maybe I got one of the rascals.

Some of the troopers on the right side of our perimeter came running toward us, and that left the whole right side completely open. Another "burp gun" fired from that direction,

*A rear view from our positions at O'Connel Pass near the Imjin River, December 1951, just before a 10-inch snowstorm.*

which could only mean one thing — they were coming after us from two sides. What worried me was the fact they could be behind us. If they were, we were in deep trouble. Lieutenant Robertson had only a few seconds to decide what to do. With the whole platoon in disarray, he had only one option and that was to get out in a hurry. With the whole right side of our perimeter gone, it left the Lieutenant no choice. Everyone started back down the slope, and Lieutenant Robertson told me to bring up the rear and try to slow down the Chinese with my automatic carbine.

I tried to find a BAR man to help, but in the darkness and confusion I couldn't find anyone. It didn't take but a few seconds for everyone to clear out, so I started backing down the hill as fast as I could. What should have been an organized retreat turned into an all-out race for the river. The Chinese were pressing in for the kill. I could see them on both my right and my left. They were trying to slam the door on some of us, and we had to get out before it slammed. We almost waited too long. I was forced to break into a run the last 100 yards to the river. I could have killed several of them, but I decided against it. To stop and try to make a fight of it now would be suicide. At the moment I didn't know where the rest of the platoon was. All I could see in the moonlight was Chinese soldiers trying to catch up with the others and me. I kept wondering why they were not firing at me — then the chilling truth registered. They probably had in mind taking me prisoner if they could, and killing me would be a last resort. It was also possible they didn't realize they had me cornered. As far as I could tell, I was alone and like a hunted animal.

I found myself standing on a 30-foot cliff next to the river. I had missed the place where we had come up earlier that evening. What a stupid stunt, and it could cost me my life. I had already decided I would rather die than be taken prisoner. Death would be better than a North Korean prison camp. I flattened out on the ground and tried to decide what to do. In the darkness I could see figures moving on my right and more on my left.

So this was it. This was how a 20-year-old kid from South Missouri was going to die. A feeling of bitterness came over me, and my thoughts drifted back home. The sickening truth of the situation was overwhelming. I wondered if Eva, my wife, was praying for me right now. I wondered if somehow she knew what I had gotten into. At the moment the Chinese were getting closer, it was time to decide what to do.

At this moment my whole life flashed before me, and I knew I had only a few seconds to make up my mind. I had three options: go over the cliff and hope I didn't kill myself. Be taken prisoner, or fight it out with them, which at the moment I didn't intend to do (I would have as a last resort if I had to). Lying flat on the ground I made my decision; I crawled over to the cliff and feet first slid over the edge. I reached out and desperately grabbed for anything that would slow down my fall. Amazingly, I latched onto what seemed like a grapevine and began to lower myself down toward the bottom of the cliff. Luckily the vines hung nearly all the way to the bottom. About 10 feet above a small 10-foot wide sandbar, I hesitated before I dropped from the vines. Several weeks ago I had listened to other troopers tell about the quicksand in this river. If this was quicksand below me, I was a cooked goose. Before I turned loose of the vines, I prayed to God that the sandbar below me was not quicksand. When I landed I knew that once again God had answered my prayers. Down the river I could see where the sandbar widened, and I realized that was the direction I would have to go to get back where we had crossed earlier that night. I could hear the Chinese talking above me on the bluff. I knew that I had to get going fast.

At that particular moment I was hidden in the darkness near the bluff, but down the river about 50 yards I would be completely in the open on the 50-foot wide sandbar we had come up earlier. It was my only way out and I had to take it! The talking above me had stopped, so I decided this was it. I unstrapped my carbine from around my neck and shoulder and pushed the lever on the side to full automatic. I no longer had any options. I had to make it back to where we crossed the river or not make it at all.

About the time I made my move the moon went behind a cloud and turned the place into total darkness. What a break! I prayed it would stay dark until I got back across the river. As I charged down the sandbar, I fully expected the Chinese to open fire. Luckily they didn't. When I got to where I would wade across the river, the moon came out from behind the clouds and lit the place up like it was daytime. Why they didn't open fire on me I'll never know. I felt like a setting duck. About then my platoon medic joined me, and we hit the water and started wading across. Most of the platoon was already across, and just when I thought we were home free a rifle fired from behind us and I heard the unmistakable "splat" of lead against flesh. The medic went down in the water, shot through the stomach. Our luck had finally ran out, and I knew I would be next. The rifle fired again, and I heard the slug snap past my head. The medic was still struggling in the water and trying to keep from floating down the river. As bad as he was wounded, he would drown for sure. Lieutenant Robertson screamed at me to go get him. I jumped back in the water and waded out to where he was. I grabbed him by the arm and started back to the bank. About then another trooper ran out and helped me drag him to safety. Before we got back to the bank, the rifle fired again. I flinched, but the bullet snapped past us and we were home free. The big medic was bleeding from the wound, and the pain was awful. We gave him morphine for the pain and wrapped the wound with bandages.

Lieutenant Robertson called artillery on to the other side of the river, and for five minutes they blasted the whole area. This was the first time we had been able to call in support fire. I'm sure the Chinese paid a big price this night (at least I hope they did). I checked with all the squad leaders to make sure everybody was accounted for. The medic was the only one who was wounded, but one of our ROK soldiers was missing, and we had to assume he was dead or taken prisoner. Frankly, I was amazed we didn't lose all or half of the platoon this night. We waited for a half-hour to see if the missing ROK soldier would return. He never did.

We put our wounded medic on a stretcher and headed back to our line. All of us knew what a bad night this had been, and not a word was spoken all the way back. All you could hear were the groans of the medic. By the time we got back he was spitting up blood and was as white as a sheet. Lord, I felt sorry for him. His religious belief demanded that he not carry a gun of any kind. I had been on his case for a month to at least carry a "45 pistol" for a little protection. He flatly refused until this patrol when I finally got him to carry a carbine. The last thing he said to me before they carried him away was, "Sarge, I told you I shouldn't carry a weapon." I felt like a bum, and I swore I would never try to get anyone else to carry a weapon against his will as long as I was platoon sergeant of this platoon. I deeply regretted losing the big guy; he was the best medic I had in all my time in Korea. Sadly, I would never see him again. I felt guilty for a month about having him carry a carbine.

**********

It was beginning to get daylight by the time I got back to our CP. Lieutenant Robertson decided to go on up to the company CP and report the night's happenings on our patrol. I didn't try to go eat chow; I was completely worn out from our ordeal across the Imjin River. Frankly, I hoped it would be our last time for a while to get that close to the enemy's front door. A lot of second-guessing took place about our disorganized retreat. The truth of the matter was simply the fact that we were too far from our line with too little help to make a fight of it. I for one agreed with Lieutenant Robertson.

We had to get out when we did. If we had dug in our heels and stayed put, without a doubt I firmly believe we would have all been killed or captured. In my opinion the whole operation was a fiasco. We could have stayed and fought it out with them, and no doubt, we could have killed a bunch of them, but being that close to their line they would have finally overwhelmed us with manpower which they had by the thousands. You can't carry enough ammunition to kill them all. Frankly, I think they let us get as close as we did so they could surround us and wipe us out. That is the Chinese way to do things. Had we got some men hit before we got back to the

*Master Sergeant Denzil Batson with carbine and 2nd Lieutenant Ralph Robertson near the 2nd Platoon C.P., December 1951, south of the Imjin River.*

river, we would have been in deep trouble. It could have been a big disaster. The truth of the matter was, the right flank of our perimeter caved in, and when that happened we had no choice but to get out.

The very next night we went on patrol again, only this time we didn't cross the river. On our way back to the MLR we spotted a wooden stake driven into the ground alongside the path. On top of the stake was a Christmas card. After we made sure it wasn't rigged to a "booby trap," I opened the Christmas card and in the moonlight I could clearly read, "Merry Christmas, GI's." It was signed "The Chinese People's Army." In the next several days we found several Christmas cards. A lot of them told us we should surrender and join the Communists. All the troops in the 2nd Platoon had their own special "words" for the Chinese. None of them was what you would put on a Christmas card.

**********

The days of mid-December dragged slowly by, and life in the

bunkers became routinely boring. One morning about daylight the Chinese threw in some mortar fire, and Lieutenant Nicoli, the 3rd Platoon leader, was standing outside his bunker and was killed by the flying shrapnel. He hadn't been in Korea but a short time. I stood and watched as some of his men carried him down the hill. That's how it was on the front line in Korea. Some died and some went on living, at least until the next bullet or the next artillery or mortar round found its mark. I felt sorry for him and for his family that would be getting the sad news in a few days.

One morning I woke up and found that it had snowed about 10 inches during the night. The white stuff blanketed the hills of Korea and for the first time this place looked almost beautiful. Of course, the white snow and the fact that Christmas was almost here stirred the homesickness that was in the heart of every man on the hill. At times like this it was easy for the loneliness to get to you. I learned to always try and stay busy doing something to make the time go by faster and to keep my morale up. Besides, I was getting a lot of mail from home, and that was the big thing that kept me going, especially the letters from my wife.

In a couple of days some of the snow melted. In a few more days it had gotten a little colder, so it looked like some of the white stuff would be with us for awhile. One day about noon we got the word that battalion had decided to send another patrol across the Imjin River. This time it would be the 1st Platoon. We were told to stay on the alert and be ready to assist them if they got into trouble. As far as I was concerned, there would be no doubt about them getting into trouble. On the way back to our Platoon CP from the chow area that evening, I told Lieutenant Robertson that I was going to let everyone know right now what might be coming later that night. He agreed, so I went around to all our positions and informed all the squad leaders to get everyone ready to move out, just in case we were called on.

When I told the men what could happen and where we might have to go, one of them said to me, "Sarge, where was all the help the night we crossed the river?"

I tried to ignore what he said but deep down I knew exactly

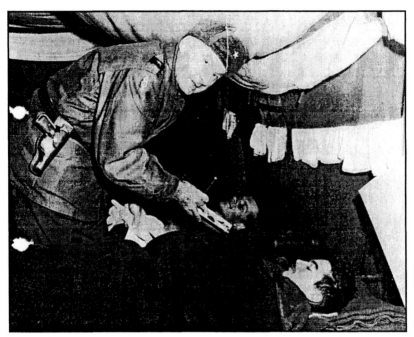

*William C. Moore being presented the Purple Heart by Commanding General of the 3rd Division, Thomas Cross. The man in the background was wounded at the same time as Moore, at the Imjin River.*

how he felt. When I got back to the CP, I told Lieutenant Robertson someone had asked me about the lack of help we had when we crossed the river. "By the way, sir, where was all the help that night?" The truth was we would have to get out any way we could. Getting help hadn't even been discussed. The lieutenant ignored my question.

Darkness settled in across the hills, and the 1st Platoon was getting ready for their patrol across the Imjin. I found a place outside the CP where I could sit down and watch the night's proceedings. After awhile the 1st Platoon left the MLR in single file and headed down the rice paddies toward the river. I didn't envy them at all. Pretty soon they disappeared in the moonlight. It would be a long night for them, a night that would almost get the 2nd Platoon involved again.

Tonight it was cold and clear. The snow was still on the ground and frozen as hard as a rock. I could hear the crunch of combat boots walking through the frozen stuff for a mile. Any ideas of being quiet this night went out the window in a hurry. Hanging in the sky out in front of me was a bright full moon, and the stars again were out by the millions. One thing for sure, as bright as the moon was shining, the 1st Platoon wouldn't have any trouble seeing where they were going. The only trouble with that the Chinese could see real well, too. I told Lieutenant Robertson a "Chinaman" could see in the dark like a cat. He looked at me for a moment and told me I had been in Korea too long.

"Sir, if that is the case, I would like to leave right now." The next look he gave me told me the conversation was over. My joke hadn't gone over too well.

After an hour or so the whole company area was as still as a mouse. The only noise was occasional outgoing artillery round fired by our big guns behind us. I began to relax and get drowsy and about the time I finally decided to go inside the CP; I heard from across the river the unmistakable bark of a "burp gun" and the chatter of a carbine. A few more shots rang out and then silence. I went inside the CP, and Lieutenant Robertson had just got the word the 1st Platoon was in trouble and needed help. It took a few minutes to alert everybody, but in a short time we were ready to go. This was going to be one hairy operation. I didn't look forward to another visit across the river. The 1st Platoon had two or three men wounded and were trying to get them out, and the Chinese were trying to stop them. A couple of the Chinese soldiers came out of nowhere and tried to drag one of the wounded troopers away, but someone else killed both of the enemy soldiers. That's how fanatical the Chinese were at times.

We had just started to leave the MLR when the word came over the radio that the 1st Platoon had made it back across the river and probably wouldn't need our help. Nevertheless, we stayed on the alert for the rest of the night. Once the 1st Platoon cleared the river, our artillery blasted the area for several minutes. I hoped they caught several of the Chinese out in the open. Lieutenant Robertson was disappointed we didn't get to help the 1st Platoon. He told me it would have been a good chance to even the score. I would have liked to even the score, but I wasn't all that thrilled about going back across the river.

\*\*\*\*\*\*\*\*\*

We had been in the area a little less than a month when the word came that another unit would relieve us and we would go into reserve. This was great news to us, but as it would turn out our reserve time

*Second Platoon members, at the Imjin River, late 1951.*

would be about a week. One good thing, we got to eat a big Christmas dinner on Christmas Day. Big tents had been set up in a small valley a few miles behind the MLR. It was nice to relax for a few days and get a shower and a clean set of clothing. Lord, we felt almost human again. As a matter of fact, on Christmas night someone came up with a guitar and mandolin again, and we sang Christmas songs until late at night. The favorite song was "Blue Christmas," and everyone would join in. By the time we finished singing, the tears were flowing freely from several of the troops. I thought the music was great. It was as good as anything you could get right out of Nashville, Tennessee.

A couple of days after Christmas the 2nd Battalion assembled down the road a ways from our tents, and one of our commanding generals came up and give us a pep talk. He informed us we would be going back to the frontline before long. This was the period of time that everyone was calling "the beginning of trench warfare." Personally, I hadn't noticed any change myself. To me and most of the troopers of the 2nd Platoon, war was war, any way you cut it. In his speech the general told us to stay alert at all times, and he wanted us to kill anything that moved. I wondered what they thought we had been doing for the past month or so.

For the next few days about all we did was eat and sleep. I guess they were getting us well rested for the months that lay ahead. Everybody had got a clean change of clothing and a new pair of boots. The clothing change would be our last for three long months. One evening Lieutenant Robertson informed me that we would be moving out the next day at noon. The reserve time we had hoped would last awhile ended in about a week. When I asked Lieutenant Robertson where we were going this time, he said it would be back to my favorite piece of real estate — Little Gibraltar Hill. We were to relieve the 7th Infantry Regiment who had been there since we had left a month ago around Thanksgiving. I passed the word on to the squad leaders, and that night before I went to sleep I took the time to write my wife a letter by the light of a candle. I wrote her and it went something like this:

*Dearest Darling,*

*Well, the time in reserve I told you about has ended after only about a week. We did have a big Christmas dinner and got a clean change of clothes, which was really great. Now we are going back to the frontline, in an area where we were in November around Thanksgiving. I'm not sure what the situation is over there, but I'm sure we can deal with it, whatever it is. Don't worry about me, I'll be just fine. I'll write to you again just as soon as I can find the time. With all my love …*

*Your husband*

**********

The next day about noon we loaded up on the trucks and headed down the road. True to form, it was cold and light drizzle was falling. It would be dark by the time we got to our destination. As the trucks rolled along, old memories began to come back about the area we were going to. I didn't look forward to this return at all, and I wondered how long we would be in this Godforsaken place. Of course, I had no way of knowing it then, but it would be a long cold four months on this hill. Men would be wounded and men would die before our stay here would end.

One thing we had going for us was the fact that a lot of us

were familiar with this place after being here during the battle for the hill in November. Before we would leave here again I would know this whole area like the back of my hand. On the darkest of nights out on patrol, I could always tell where I was by just looking at the hills and ridges that lay in the no-man's land between us and the Chinese. To me, it was an advantage to know the area. In the months to come all the above would be important to us, as the 2nd Platoon would be the sacrificial lamb on most patrols in this area. When our time here was over, our number in the 2nd Platoon would be smaller than ever before.

********

On the ride over to Little Gibraltar Hill I had time to reflect on our three-week stay at O'Conell Pass. The one thing that stuck in my craw was the patrol that we went out on across the Imjin River. It wasn't the fact that we beat a hasty retreat that bothered me, but pure and simple, we should have inflicted heavy casualties on them while we retreated. I personally could have killed a bunch of them; yet I elected not to because I didn't know where the rest of the platoon was at that moment. One of my biggest fears was killing some of our own people by mistake. Had a bunch of us started firing on the Chinese, they might have had second thoughts about pressing us all the way back to the river. Several of the troops told me that they couldn't tell who the Chinese were or who the GI's were and that's why they didn't start firing. When it's dark it's hard to tell who is friend and who is foe. I could understand that because I found myself in the same situation. I made a vow that next time it would be different. We would all get our chance again in the coming weeks. I would always regret that we didn't make them pay the night across the Imjin River.

**********

Our stay at the Imjin River positions had been less than a month, but it had cost the company several more men, and this time, at least for the time being, there wouldn't be any replacements. Our number had shrunk by at least a dozen men. The 2nd Platoon was lucky this time. We had lost only three people. The 1st and 3rd Platoons had lost more people than we did. That's how it was on the frontline. You never knew if the next time would be your turn or someone else's. Such is the life of the "dog face" infantryman. The pressure is always with you, and if you want to stay alive you learn to never relax. Even when I went to sleep at night, my bed partner was my M-2 carbine. Of course, an infantryman's bed was a hole in the ground, sometimes with three inches of water in the bottom. Everywhere I went, my M-2 carbine was fully loaded. You took care of your weapon like it was a baby. All the troops in the 2nd Platoon did exactly that. A man would be a fool not to take care of his weapon on the frontline in Korea. It could mean life or death at any time. All of the above would shortly be put to the test on our return to Little Gibraltar Hill. The one thing I didn't know was just how "stiff" the test would be. We would find out in the cold months that lay ahead. When we had left this area a month ago, I had asked myself the question, would I ever see this place again. That was being answered now. The trucks came to a halt, and directly in front of us outlined against the dark night sky was Little Gibraltar Hill.

# CHAPTER 4

# Return to Little Gibraltar Hill

THE NIGHT WAS AS BLACK as the ace of spades. It was as cold as a witch's heart when we reached the road to the back of Little Gibraltar Hill. We unloaded from the trucks and tried to assemble together at the side of the road. In the total darkness it was difficult to do, but after an hour or so of mass confusion we finally got it all sorted out and moved into our new positions replacing elements of the 7th Regiment on and around Little Gibraltar Hill. The area for "F" Company was on the right of the big hill on a low ridgeline that extended about 500 yards to the east. "E" Company was on the high part of Little Gibraltar Hill and "G" Company on the left side. As in the last position at the Imjin River, the 2nd Platoon was located in the middle of the company perimeter defense. Our trench-line, bunkers and fighting holes were almost down to the rice paddies that fronted our position and extended several hundred yards directly to our front. On our left was the 1st Platoon which extended a short distance up the hill and tied in with "E" Company. The 3rd Platoon was on our right and on a slightly higher ridge than we were. To the 3rd Platoon's right was an open rice paddy about 400 hundred yards wide, and beyond that one of our other units was dug in on line.

After awhile we all found out where we were supposed to go, thanks to a Sergeant who was left here by the 7th Regiment to guide us into our positions. I always wondered just what would happen during a changeover if the Chinese decided to attack at that time. I hoped it would never happen, and this time it didn't.

By the time Lieutenant Robertson and I had checked on the entire Platoon and got our sound power phones tied in to all the squad leaders, I was almost totally exhausted. When we got into our Platoon CP, Lieutenant Robertson told me to get some sleep and he would take the first watch. I was glad to hear this, so when I stretched out on a sleeping bag it wasn't long until I was totally sound asleep. This begins a four-month stretch that would take its toll on all of us before we would see any more reserve time.

The last few months of 1951 had been a rough time for all of us, and 1952 wouldn't be any better. Had I known what lay ahead, I might not have slept so soundly. Death would stalk this hill again, and some of the 2nd Platoon would be the victims. It was a never-ending cycle, and before it ended the 2nd Platoon would be smaller in number than ever before. Every man in the platoon hoped that this time on the line wouldn't be his time to be killed or wounded, but sadly, it would be for some. The menu would be a steady diet of "contact and ambush" patrols that, as far as I'm concerned, are every bit as dangerous, or more so, than an all-out attack. The 2nd Platoon would get more than its share of action. It would start the next night in a cold drizzle and fog.

**********

Daylight came the first morning with light drizzle falling, and a heavy fog hung over the hills and rice paddies of Korea. It was cold and damp, but all the troops had been issued winter clothing so we were in pretty good shape to withstand the cold weather. That morning the cooks had prepared hot chow and brought it up to the road behind the hill and served us a few at a time. The hot food and coffee really hit the spot, and most of us ate like pigs. It was a credit to our cooks that they could prepare hot chow and bring it up to the front.

In the daylight we could better see what our positions looked like. To our front a small hill rose out of the rice paddies. We would use this small hill for an "OP" or outpost, and we would man it every night with a squad of 2nd Platoon troopers. Past this small hill the rice paddies continued for a hundred yards and then gave way to a long ridgeline a quarter-mile long that ran east to west that was called "Crete." This long ridgeline was the halfway point between the Chinese and us. On the backside of Crete were more rice paddies and then more hills, the highest being "317" which was held by the Chinese. A long ridgeline ran from the top of "317" to the west which was also held by the Chinese. The "no man's land" that lay between the two armies would be the battle ground for a lot of clashes, mostly at night, before our stay here was over. These clashes would be short and bloody. Whichever side caught the other in the open was usually the winner.

The 7th Regiment had laid a minefield in the rice paddies in front of our positions, but we had a safe lane marked across it with white tape that glowed in the darkness so we could see it day or night when we were out on patrol. They also had strung barbwire across the company front, and later on we added five-gallon napalm cans with a quick fuse wire tied to a stake. If the wire was pulled slightly, the napalm can would explode, and the burning red stuff would shower anyone close to it. This would mean a horrible death for the victim. It was also dangerous business to set these napalm cans. One slip and that would be the end. Also, we tied tin cans to the barbed wire so that if someone hit the wire the cans would rattle and warn us if someone was approaching our line. Sometimes the wind would blow and cause the cans to rattle, which would cause a false alarm. We didn't mind this because in a matter of life and death any little bit of help was welcome. The false alarms helped to keep us alert at all times. You never knew if the wind or the Chinese caused the cans to rattle.

About noon the fog began to lift and we could get even a closer view of the surrounding terrain in every direction. The small hill that lay 400 yards to our front was a point of interest to us, so Lieutenant Robertson decided to check it out. One of our squads would be on this hill as a listening post the coming night, so we wanted to know what it looked like up close. Lieutenant Robertson told me to tag along. The two of us left the MLR and headed out the safe lane toward the small hill. In the rice paddies on both sides of our safe lane were several dead Chinese lying around. I asked Lieutenant Robertson if he thought I should shoot all of them again just to be sure they were dead. He stopped and looked at me as if I had lost it — then he realized I was being funny and continued on toward the hill.

Shortly we began to climb the hill and, frankly, I was a little bit nervous. This was our first time out here and you never knew what could happen. When we got to the top, there were more dead Chinese laying around and some of them were still standing up in the fighting holes they were killed in. The dead Chinese bodies were frozen stiff by the cold Korean winter winds. These Chinese troopers had been killed back in November when we had taken Little Gibraltar Hill. Now I could see up close what our artillery and small arms fire had done to them. These dead bodies would be here for the next two or three months until warm weather began to thaw them out. The stink would be almost unbearable. Several fighting holes had been dug around the top of the hill, so that meant our troops wouldn't have to dig any holes. The only thing was all the holes were already occupied by dead Chinese troopers. Lieutenant Robertson remarked to me that our men would always have company even though they were dead and frozen stiff. I wasn't sure that I thought that was funny. He reminded me that my earlier remark about shooting people didn't sound any better than his remark. I couldn't argue with that.

A long ridgeline extended from the top of our outpost hill and gradually sloped down to the rice paddies in the valley floor to the west. Lieutenant Robertson and I agreed this would be the most likely route of approach to the top of the hill and we would inform our squad leaders of this fact when we returned. Just to the north of where we were was the long ridgeline Crete, and past it were more hills that rose to another high ridgeline that ran all the way to the top of hill "317" which was held by the Chinese. Behind us where "E" Company was deployed, you could see the rugged and solid rock outline of Little Gibraltar Hill looming higher than any other hill in the area. I could clearly see the twin peaks outlined in the sky. Old memories came flooding back, and I pointed out Peak III to Lieutenant Robertson where we had spent a long day and night back in late November. Now I know how the hill looked to the Chinese when they were attacking. On the back of Little Gibraltar you could see other dead Chinese soldiers still lying where they had fallen during the November battle. To our west, in the rice paddies, other dead bodies were scattered around. What a price they had paid, but to the Chinese a man's life didn't mean much. When they attacked, they came after you in droves. Sometimes you couldn't stack up enough ammunition to kill them all. A lot of them didn't even carry a weapon when they were attacking, but they all carried hand grenades.

*********

After a while we decided we had better get back to our MLR. I was a little bit surprised we hadn't been fired on yet. We started down the hill to the safe lane, and all of a sudden a mortar round slammed into the

*Sgt. Marquis and Ken Whitteaker with rifle, at the front line, early 1952.*

rice paddies just to our left and exploded. I started to dive into a nearby hole, but Lieutenant Robertson just kept walking and didn't bat an eye. I couldn't help but admire the cold-blooded nerve of this man. I honestly believe that he wasn't afraid of anything, and more times than I could remember he had proved it. He was a "dyed in the wool" combat soldier, and I firmly believe he enjoyed every minute of combat. He told me several times not to worry about being killed and I would be a better soldier. I never did figure out a way to "not" worry about being killed. He firmly believed that if you died in battle that was the way it was supposed to be and you couldn't change that. After I thought about it for a while, I couldn't argue with what he said. The Chinese didn't throw in any more mortar rounds, but they had let us know that they were watching our every move. We got back to the MLR without further problems. Usually the Chinese won't fire on one or two people, but any more than that they really go after you. They could drop a mortar round in your back pocket.

Late that evening the fog began to move in again, but the rain clouds had begun to break up, and when it got dark a pale moon would break through the clouds and give the fog an eerie look. We waited until about 9 o'clock before we sent the second squad out to man the outpost. I told the squad leader, Don Marcelli, about the outpost hill and to be alert and expect anything. He was a good soldier, and I doubt he needed my advice but he assured me he would be careful. They would be in contact with us by sound power phone. I told Marcelli I would be standing by with the rest of the platoon in case he needed help.

By the time they had started out the safe lane, he had a pretty good idea of what to expect. I went down to the bunker line to see them off, and I watched them disappear into the fog. I went back to our CP where I could listen in to all the conversations that took place and to keep up on what was happening. It wasn't long until Marcelli came on the phone and informed us that the Chinese had set a "booby trap" in the safe lane, and by pure luck they had seen the copper wire that was stretched across the safe lane about ankle high. The man who saw the copper wire was a tall, skinny kid from Kentucky by the name of Miller. We called him "bird dog." He could smell a Chinaman a mile away.

Now the task faced the squad leader on what to do about the booby trap. Along the safe lane earlier that day we had seen some old como wire that had been strung along on the ground. By cutting a 20-foot-long piece of this como wire, they slipped one end under the copper wire, looped it over the top and tied it. From behind a bank at the edge of the rice paddies, they jerked the wire and exploded the booby trap. From 75 yards away on top of the outpost hill the Chinese opened fire on the squad. It was an attempt at an ambush. They almost pulled it off. After an exchange of fire that lasted only a few minutes, Lieutenant Robertson ordered Marcelli to assault the hill. They charged to the top, only to find that the Chinese had bugged out down the back slope.

While all this was going on, I had alerted the rest of the platoon to be ready to go to the aid of Marcellli's squad. As a matter of fact, the whole company was alerted in case the Chinese were up to something big. We stayed on the alert all night, but nothing else happened.

At daylight the squad returned to the MLR, and Marcelli checked in with Lieutenant Robertson and then along with the rest of the Squad were told to get some much-needed sleep.

So, the first day and night here had been an exciting one, one of many that lay ahead for us. We praised the squad for being alert enough to spot the booby trap. If they had not seen the wire across the path, Marcelli would probably have been killed and others most likely killed or wounded. One month later Marcelli would die as a result of stepping on a mine. What a sad ending for a great soldier who was also a good friend of mine. It would be for me, personally, a bitter pill to swallow, when he died.

**********

The early days of January 1952 was a time of change for "F" Company and the 2nd Platoon. Five or six of the old veterans who had been in Korea for a long time were rotated home. I had been with most of them for three or four months, and I very much hated to see them go. I was glad for them that they had made it through. They were one happy bunch when I went down to inform them to get ready to leave. The next day we got three or four new replacements, and they sort of took up the space left by the departing veterans. Our company commander who had been with us for three months also left the company and was replaced by a new man who was a captain.

One morning the new company commander called our CP and informed us that the tank company was sending a "Patton tank" up to the front and they would place it close to the 2nd Platoon CP, which, of course, would give us more fire-power on the line. The road that curved around the backside of Little Gibraltar Hill had been improved to the point as to allow tanks to move into the MLR. The next morning when the tank arrived, they brought with them a shower of mortar fire from the Chinese. I told Lieutenant Robertson I wasn't sure I liked our new neighbor very much. Later on in the weeks ahead these tankers would be my best support fire, especially in daylight action. The tank commander was a man that you could count on, and I would find that out before long.

**********

The one man in "F" Company that I looked up to more than anyone else was my First Sergeant, Robert O. Hunter. He was a veteran of World War II and was always as upbeat as anyone could be. He was a real character and was as dependable as could be. As I have said before, Hunter helped me out in a lot of ways. When I first arrived in Korea, I was one scared kid, so it was good for me to be around a man like Hunter who could give you the appearance of being calm and cool at all times and a man who could laugh at anything. Through it all he was a great soldier and first sergeant.

I can remember one night in particular I went on a patrol with my 2nd Platoon and we were to go out to the horseshoe hill on the west end of the ridgeline crete and set up an ambush in the hopes of killing Chinese or maybe taking a prisoner. It was a cold, clear night, the moon was out, and we were set up in our perimeter defense, and the long night began. It was so still you could hear a pin drop. Over just to the north of us in the hills you could hear a bunch of Chinese talking back and forth to each other. They sounded like they were in the process of digging new positions. Talking as low as I could, I reported back to the CO what we were hearing. We were told to ignore it unless they became a threat to us. It was then that First Sergeant Hunter came on the radio and played me part of the Earnest Tubb tune that he was picking up from a radio station in Japan. As still as the night was, I was convinced that the Chinese could hear the radio going. I had to laugh, but some of the guys told me in no uncertain terms to" turn that radio off, Sarge, are you trying to get us killed?"

When I got back to the company area, I checked in at the company C.P. Hunter and I had a big laugh out of the music he played me that night on patrol. The name of the song was

"Blue Christmas," my favorite. The next day some officer from Battalion came up the road in a jeep and stopped at my platoon C.P. The first thing he said was, "Man, I sure enjoyed that music I heard on the radio last night. Sergeant, I don't guess you know how that happened, do you?"

On the left holding carbine is Lt. Wright, 1st Platoon. Standing next to jeep, Master Sergeant Robert O. Hunter, first sergeant of "F" Company.

"Sir, I sure don't, it just all of a sudden started playing on my radio, and I can't tell you where it came from."

He looked at me for a moment and said, "Sarge, you are a pretty good liar," and with that he drove on down the road.

The month of January dragged on, and so did the war. Instead of all-out attacks and taking more ground, the fighting had slowed down to an exchange of artillery and mortar fire and platoon and squad-size patrols mostly at night. They were bloody and vicious, and casualties were the order of the day. Both sides had dug in deeper and had brought up more firepower to inflict more casualties on each other. All this became the everyday life style of the "dog face infantrymen." The 2nd Platoon had more than its share of patrols, and the casualties were a constant thorn in the side. At one time during the last part of January we were down to 20 men in the platoon. A few days later we got back some troopers who had been only slightly wounded. I was glad to get them back.

One Sunday morning the last part of January I was told by the 1st sergeant that our Protestant chaplain was coming up to the front to hold church services behind the hill where we went to eat chow. It had been a while since we had been able to have church services. I went down and told all the squad leaders to send anyone down to the service who wanted to go. It was well attended. I walked down with some of the troops to hear the chaplain speak. He was a major and neatly dressed, making us infantrymen look like ragged bums. One of the guys sitting next to me leaned over and remarked to me that the man looked "like a sissy." At that moment while the chaplain was speaking, three or four mortar rounds slammed in around us and exploded. Everyone dived into a hole or behind a rock. The chaplain didn't bat an eye and didn't even move. He kept reading his Bible and acted as if nothing had ever happened. So much for the remark that he was a sissy. When the service was over, we were a red-faced bunch of troops. From that day on all of us showed him nothing but the utmost respect. When I told Lieutenant Robertson what had happened, he laughed until he almost cried. I had the feeling that the chaplain also had a big laugh at the expense of the 2nd Platoon. After I thought about what he done, I wondered if it was being brave or just plain stupid.

* * * * * * * *

February came in like a roaring lion. It snowed quite a bit and was bitterly cold. The peace talks had slowed to a snail's pace, and most of us could see no hope of the war ending. We figured the only way out of Korea was to be killed or wounded or finally make it out on rotation — if you lived long enough. Several had made it through, so we had to remain hopeful that we would someday do the same.

One day our 1st sergeant was sent home on an emergency leave. He had joined the company the same day I did, and we were the best of friends. He had been a lot of help to me, and I deeply dreaded to see him go. The day he left he stopped by the 2nd Platoon CP to tell me good-bye. We shook hands, and he told me to "stay healthy and take care of myself." I couldn't believe he was leaving. Pretty soon he just turned and walked away. I would never see him again. We had just lost the best 1st sergeant I seen while I was in Korea.

The platoon sergeant of the 4th Platoon took over as 1st sergeant. One of his squad leaders took over the 4th Platoon. Changes like this would happen several times more before my time in Korea was over.

That day we got in a few more replacements which was always a welcome sight. A few of them joined the 2nd Platoon and were spread out in each of the squads, which were still short several men. Even with the new guys we were only about three-fourths strength. Of course, every time we got new men, we always seemed to lose others, so it was a never-ending cycle. We just had to make out with what we had. One of the new replacements was a SFC and was a veteran of World War II. I talked Lieutenant Robertson into making him the assistant platoon sergeant. It turned out to be a good move. SFC Ledger was one of the best men I ever had in the Platoon CP. We worked together well, and he really took a lot of pressure off me.

**********

What I considered as one of the most dangerous patrols I ever went on while in Korea occurred the first week in February. We didn't fire a shot. There was still a lot of snow on the ground and the weather was as cold as the North Pole. Lieutenant Robertson called me from the company CP and told me he wanted to see me shortly about a patrol that we would have to go on that night. When I heard all the details from him, the thought crossed my mind, "Who came up with this brainstorm?" He showed me a map overlay and pointed out three check points where we were to go and report any enemy activity that might be going on. The farthest place we would go and the nearest to the Chinese line was at the foot of "317." We would be dangerously close to the Chinese front door. He told me to take only four or five men and warned me not to get into any firefights with a large unit of Chinese. If we ran into trouble, we were to get out in a hurry. Our main purpose was to find out if they were digging any big gun emplacements or bunkers on or around any of the three points that were our objective north of the ridgeline Crete. Scanning the area with field glasses, you could see that from Crete over to the foot of "317" was nothing but rice paddies. Once you reached the foot of "317," it become fairly well covered with scrub-brush and small timber that was thick enough to hide either a bunker or gun emplacement. This was the reason for us going out to see close up if we could find out what was going on.

When I asked what would happen if we got hit hard that far from our line, no one would give me any assurance that we would get any help. The plain truth was we would be completely on our own. If anything happened it was simple — we would have to get out any way we could. Sergeant Ledger and I agreed that if, in fact, we did get hit, our chances of getting back at all were slim and none. When I went down to the troops on line and asked for four volunteers and related to them the facts of our patrol, not one of them failed to volunteer. By the time it got dark we were ready to go.

A bright moon was out and the sky was clear and it was bitterly cold. The snow on the ground was frozen hard as a rock. We left the MLR, and once we cleared the safe lane we turned northeast and headed for Crete that loomed ahead in the moonlight. My radioman was staying close to me, and he was carrying a "walkie-talkie" radio instead of the bigger box-like radio that was bigger and heavier and harder to carry. We didn't want any excess weight to slow us down this night. We didn't want the excess weight, but the small radio didn't work very well. I hoped it would tonight. At the top of Crete I called Lieutenant Robertson and told him our location. He informed me then that any patrol we might run into would be Chinese, as no American units had anyone out this night. I thanked him for the information and we continued down the back slope of Crete.

Once we got to the bottom of the hill and started across the rice paddies toward "317," I was a bundle of nerves. It was impossible not to make noise walking on the frozen snow. The night was still and it seemed to me like you could hear a pin drop. A slight breeze rustled the scrub-brush just ahead, and we were just a few yards away from our objective. You could smell Chinese all over the place, and every time the breeze stirred it was even stronger. For the life of me I couldn't see where they had been doing any digging at all, but there was no doubt they had a listening post here. As close as we were to them, I was amazed that they didn't open fire on us. I signaled for the men to halt and we crouched down in the scrub brush. I fully expected a hail of small arms fire, but it didn't happen.

*Left to right: Lt. Ralph Robertson, Captain Luke, Lt. Wright and Lt. Morndort, "F" Company officers, near hill "355" in early 1952.*

I whispered to Sergeant Ledger to start back the way we had come and I would bring up the rear. Every second we stayed here now put us nearer a disaster. About 20 yards up the top of the ridge I could see two Chinese soldiers standing in a fighting hole. It was a miracle they hadn't heard us walking on the frozen snow. We didn't waste any time moving back across the rice paddies to Crete. When we got back to the top of the ridgeline, I breathed a sigh a relief. We hit the other check-points and found nothing. I was completely worn out, and I called Lieutenant Robertson and informed him we were heading home. A half-hour later we entered our safe lane and the safety of our MLR. The next morning I told the company commander the only thing we saw on the ridge at "317" was an outpost. We could see no evidence of anything else.

The day came in early February when Lieutenant Robertson was to leave and go home to the U.S. What can you say to a man after you have been together for three months and been through all the things we had? When he left I felt like I had lost my right arm. The one man that I had so much confidence in and looked up to for advice would no longer be around. The responsibility of the platoon was up to me now, and that was enough to scare me to death. The night he left we shook hands, and he told me to do my best with the platoon. He turned and walked away to the jeep that would take him back to the rear and shortly disappeared in the darkness. The loneliness crushed down on me like a ton of bricks. I would never see him again. I had just lost one of the best officers I was ever around while in Korea. To say that I would miss him would be a big understatement. The next morning the company commander called and informed me that I would be the platoon leader until we got another officer to replace Robertson. In the next two weeks I found out how it was to do the job of an infantry officer. I was doing the job as a master sergeant and found out real quick it was a different ball game than being the platoon sergeant. When it came time to make a decision, it was up to me and I couldn't rely on Lieutenant Robertson to make it for me. He wasn't around any more. In the next several weeks I would grow up a lot before we left the front line.

**********

One night in mid-February I decided I would take a squad out and man the outpost for a night. I told the squad leader to stay back at the line and I would take his place for one night on the outpost. I left Sergeant Ledger in charge of the rest of the platoon, and we headed out the safe lane to our destination. I had about six men with me, and that meant we would have to set up a tight and small perimeter defense around the top of the hill. It was already dark, and we approached the outpost with extreme caution. The only enemy there was the dead ones who had been there for weeks. We each found a fighting hole to get in, and the long night began. The moon was out and it was cold, and quite a bit of snow remained on the ground. The bright moon made it easy to see, and it reflected brightly off the snow. All around our perimeter were small scrub trees and fairly thick underbrush. The bad thing about that was it would allow someone to crawl up close to us without being seen. Standing in this fighting hole with two dead Chinese and watching for some live ones to show wasn't really a pleasant way to spend the night, but it was all just routine for an infantryman. One thing I noticed about one of the two dead Chinese standing next to me in the fighting hole was a pair of bright gold teeth in front that glittered in the moonlight.

After a while all of us began to hear movement down at the foot of the hill. We were cocked and primed for a fight. I quickly notified the company commander that we had some activity going on in the valley below us. He ordered us back to the MLR. The whole company was alerted just in case the Chinese were up to something, but again the night passed without any kind of an attack being launched. A daylight patrol the next morning revealed that the Chinese had been on the prowl that night in the valley just beyond our outpost. It was hard to tell how large a force it was, but no doubt it could have given my small group a hard time if we tangled with them. Deep down I was glad the company commander had ordered us back when he did. We could have been in for a long night.

The next night the 3rd Platoon ran into a buzz saw! On the west end of Crete a horseshoe-shaped hill sort of tied into the ridgeline, and it was here the Chinese had set up an ambush. They waited until the 3rd Platoon got inside the curve of the horseshoe and opened fire from three sides. Sergeant Drummond, the platoon sergeant, asked for help, and we (2nd Platoon) got ready to go in a hurry. When we reached the top of the outpost hill, you could see the red and green tracer bullets flying through the sky like fireflies. It didn't take an expert to tell the 3rd Platoon was in one big fight.

The firing all of a sudden began to slow down, and Sergeant Drummond reported they were coming out. The Chinese had apparently called off the fight and were retreating back to their line. I heard the Artillery FO on the radio giving a fire order. In a few seconds our artillery was blasting all the area around the horseshoe hill. The company commander ordered us back to the MLR, and the 3rd Platoon was to follow us back. Amazingly they had only three or four casualties. Sergeant Drummond told me later he couldn't believe that only four people were hit.

The next night the company commander sort of gave the 2nd and 3rd Platoon a night off from patrol action. Sergeant Drummond, the 3rd Platoon sergeant, came down to my

Platoon CP, and we spent almost all night talking about the happenings of the past few weeks. After a while our conversation turned to home and family. It was daylight by the time he left for his 3rd Platoon CP. Both of us were trying to do the job of an officer in our platoon, so we had a lot in common. We had both joined "F" Company in October and were on our fifth month in Korea. We had joined the Company with 30 other people, and we were the only ones left from that group of 30.

**********

Along toward the last week in February, we got another company commander. At the same time we got a new officer for the 2nd Platoon. He had never been in combat. The company commander informed me that the new officer would take over as platoon leader and I would revert back to being the platoon sergeant. He was supposed to take out some patrols on his own, and I was told to stay out of his way and let him sort of get some "on the job training." After being in the platoon for so long and going through so much with all the men, I did a slow burn and let the CO know that I really didn't like playing second fiddle to a new man — especially someone who had never been in combat. If you didn't know the danger that existed on the frontline and if you didn't know where the minefields were and didn't know the terrain, especially at night, you were flirting with disaster. To throw a new man into a situation like that was completely stupid in my opinion. However, I must admit everybody has to start somewhere. It was up to me to help him out. When I got to Korea, I had to learn it all the hard way with no help from anyone.

The new officer lasted less than two weeks. Before he left he led the 2nd Platoon into a minefield, and one of my best squad leaders was killed when he stepped on a mine. It was a miracle that any of them got back. The disaster I had feared happened. The way it turned out, it could have been worse than what it was.

It all started one evening when the company commander called the 2nd Platoon and told me he was sending out the platoon on patrol and that I was to stay back at the MLR and let the new officer run the show. I guess they thought I would take over and run things if I went along.

When darkness fell, I watched them leave the MLR and head out the safe lane. Don Marcelli, one of the squad leaders, told me earlier that he didn't want to go on this patrol and that he had a bad feeling about it. I tried to calm his fears, but deep down I had my own bad feelings about this operation. It would be the last patrol for Don Marcelli.

I sat with my ear glued to the radio, and I could hear every report turned in by the lieutenant. All went well until they got past the horseshoe hill on the west end of Crete. On each side of the rice paddies they were walking across were ridgelines, and it was here they walked squarely into an ambush. When the lieutenant realized what was about to happen, he led a disorganized retreat into the middle of a minefield that was clearly marked. The squad leader (Marcelli) stepped on a mine and was blown into the air. For some reason the Chinese didn't fire a shot. After much confusion one of the 2nd Platoon troopers led the way out of the minefield. An hour or so later carrying the badly injured Marcelli, they entered the safe lane leading back to the MLR.

Marcelli was lying on a stretcher when I reached him. I knelt down beside him and asked him how he was. He gave me a weak smile and said, "Sarge, I don't feel so good. I told you I had a bad feeling about tonight." He was covered with a blanket, and in the pale moonlight I could see he was as white as a sheet. I raised the blanket to see how be looked and what I saw made me want to cry. His body was soft as mush, and you could see what the exploding mine had done to him. I felt sick to my soul, and I couldn't believe he was still alive. The medics hauled him away, and before he left he reached out and shook my hand. Two days later he died. When I heard about his death, I cried like a baby. The 2nd Platoon was short one great soldier and one fine human being. I went down and told all the others about his death. No one said a word, and it was a grim bunch of 2nd Platoon troopers for the next several days. After Marcelli's death some of us got letters from his mother wanting to know how her boy had died. Her words were heartbreaking, and none of us had the guts to write and tell her what happened to him. I would regret that for a lifetime. To this day I blame myself for his death. I should have kept him back that night from going on the patrol.

That night as I sat in the Platoon CP with Sergeant Ledger my morale hit rock bottom. He sensed what I was thinking, and he gave me a 30-minute lecture and told me that getting down on myself wouldn't bring Marcelli back and wouldn't help me or any of the others in the platoon. I suddenly began to realize that life had to go on, and before long I was acting like my old self again. One thing that was different after his death, I had a scar on my soul. That's how it was on the front line in Korea. You choked down your sorrow and kept going if you could. In my case, I had lots of family back home and a wife who was standing by me. She alone in my bad times is what kept me going. If it hadn't been for her love and prayers, I doubt I would have made it through Korea.

The new officer that had led the platoon that night into the minefield all of sudden left the company, and once again I become the platoon leader of the 2nd Platoon.

**********

One evening in late February I was sitting inside the Platoon CP cleaning my M-2 Carbine, when the battalion commander came in with some sergeant who was supposed to be a fearless soldier and a demolition expert. The battalion had cooked up a patrol for the next night, and my platoon was chosen to go. The sergeant was to go along, and our goal would be to blow up some bunkers on a ridge that ran down into the valley from the top of Hill 317 held by the Chinese. This was almost exactly the same spot where I had already been on another patrol, and when I saw what the plans were, the hair stood up on the back of my neck. I told the colonel that it would be suicide to get that close to the Chinese, especially trying to blow up bunkers. My argument was that we would never get close enough to do them any damage and we would be completely out in the open and would be slaughtered if they really came after us. In my mind I had no doubt they would do just that.

"Colonel, if we blow up the bunkers as we are supposed to, we will first have to knock out a Chinese outpost that I know for sure is there. If we do that, the whole Chinese army will come after us. And if they do — God help us! We had better take a lot of first aid kits with us. Sir, in a sense we will be assaulting the Chinese MLR, and that is going to be one hairy operation."

He agreed.

Sergeant Ledger told me that I made a fine speech, "Only trouble is, Sarge, nobody is listening to you."

I lost the argument and the patrol would take place as scheduled. A frontline soldier can smell "phony" 10 miles away, and as for me, I was convinced this sergeant was as "phony" as they came. Once again, I was doing a slow burn, but this time I would go along and if things didn't suit me, I planned to change that in a hurry. I just plain didn't like this sergeant and, frankly, I had about had it with all these strutting peacocks from back in the rear. My dislike for most of them grew more and more as time passed by. After this night was over, my feelings toward them would make no change.

That night found us moving out the safe lane with the so-called demolition expert near the front of the column. When we reached the top of our 2nd Platoon outpost, the sergeant began to get nervous and started to see Chinese all over the place. Something like that happens to a man when he realizes he has bit off more than he can chew. It's easy to sit back in the rear and act big. It's another thing to come up front and do all the things you brag about. Immediately I knew I was right about this guy and before things got out of hand I planned to step in. I told him to settle down and that he was wrong about Chinese being around. I told him the only Chinese here were the dead ones that were scattered around. I couldn't believe it when he called for mortar fire on the hill, and when the shells landed they almost got some of our own people.

I got on the radio and told the Company CO what had happened and that if he wanted us to continue we would, but I would run the show. I also told him that we had made enough noise to wake up every Chinaman in the area. "Captain, the man is a phony and he's playing with the lives of the men."

After some more talk about the situation we were told to return to the MLR. I was boiling mad when we got back. I apologized to the Colonel that we didn't finish the mission. He told me that he was glad I took over a situation that could have gotten out of hand. He apologized to me for the actions of the sergeant. The next morning I told the company commander that I had never seen such a total nut as this sergeant. I can tell you for sure the rest of the platoon felt the same way I did. For the next two weeks every time I walked down to the platoon area they would ask me when I was going to dig up another demolition expert. I had a feeling the demolition sergeant had fallen from grace with the colonel. The bunkers that we were to blow up that night were knocked out with artillery fire the next day.

The first week in March was upon us, and life on the frontline had become a boring routine for us all. The patrol action had slowed down, and for the time being we were content just to hold the line. Every day that went by was more of a duel between artillery units on both sides than anything else. The peace talks were stalled again, and I for one didn't put much faith in them.

I was beginning my seventh month in Korea, and I wasn't very far from my 23rd birthday. Compared to some of these young kids, I was a grandpa. Most of them were from 17 to 18 years old. If they spent enough time in combat, it wouldn't be long until they would look like they were 40.

※※※※※※※※※※※

In a few days the routine life would change and, as usual, the 2nd Platoon would be squarely in the middle of the storm. The company commander called me up to the Company CP and told me to be ready to take out a daylight patrol the next day. We were to go out to Crete near the horseshoe hill and attempt to dig in some bunkers. Rumor had it that an attempt would be made to move the MLR out to that area. By sending one platoon out to do some digging, they would find out how the Chinese would react. The reactions from them would be swift and deadly, and the target would be the 2nd Platoon.

After I left the Company CP, I went down and informed the squad leaders to be ready to go the next morning. That night I kept my squad back at the MLR and didn't man the outpost, which resulted in a chewing out by the company commander. I shot back at him that I felt like I was capable of making a few decisions on my own. That didn't go over too well and led to more chewing out. After that was all over, we got together that

94

night and went over all the details of the coming patrol.

That evening before it got dark and prior to my conference with the company commander, I walked out to the outpost hill where I could get a better view of Crete. The place where we were to go already had some fighting holes dug around the top. That would turn out to be a plus for us, but what bothered me most was the fact that the Chinese held a ridgeline just north of Crete that was a lot higher than where we would be. That meant they could look down our throats and see every move we made. I tried to shake off the feeling of disaster, but that night I couldn't sleep a wink.

I was assured the artillery would be zeroed in on all the hills around us and would be on call anytime I needed it. Also, the tank that was back at the MLR would be available. I was told to call in all targets that I felt like would give us trouble. I assumed this meant mortars, SP guns or anything else they might use against us. It was anybody's guess what they might throw at us. This is what had me worried, especially with them holding the high ground.

A new officer had come into the company, and he was to be my next platoon leader. However, today he would stay back at the MLR and sort of look after things while I was gone. He had never been in combat, and it would not have been good to send him out on a patrol his first day here. I could well remember my first day in Korea. When I joined "F" Company in October, the mortar fire was flying thick and heavy. Nobody made any attempt to keep me out of the action.

**********

At daylight we were moving out the safe lane on our way to Crete. We passed over the outpost hill and followed the ridgeline that led west to the valley floor. Once in the valley we headed across the rice paddies to Crete.

I was amazed that we hadn't been fired on yet. We reached the foot of the ridgeline and started to the top. On the way up we sort of spread out just in case, and shortly we reached the top with no problem. We quickly formed our perimeter, and for the moment we hadn't got any hostile fire. My radioman and I found a small fighting hole just below the top of the ridge on the backside, and it was here we set up shop. It wasn't long until everybody got squared away. We had two men in every hole, and that was ideal. I reminded the troops we were supposed to start digging in and improve the fighting holes that were already here. I had my radioman report back to the CO what was going on.

So far all was quiet so I walked over to the front side of the hill to see how everybody was making it. Just when I thought things might go pretty well, all hell broke loose. Machine gun fire ripped all around us, and mortar rounds were exploding all over the place. I crawled to my fighting hole where the radio was with machine gun fire hitting all round me. Everybody jumped into a hole, and amazingly no one got hit. I yelled into the radio that we were being hit, and almost instantly our artillery fire came screaming in over us and landed in the valley below us. I quickly called for them to stop firing because the small group of Chinese who had emerged from a small cave to assault our position disappeared back where they came from. But now they were pouring on the mortar and machine gunfire from the high ridge to the north. The machine gun fire was deadly, and every time someone tried to raise up they would open fire. The truth of the matter was simple — we were pinned down, and until the machine gun was knocked out we would continue to be pinned down. I had to get the machine gun located, so I crawled to the top of the ridge to see if I could locate it. When I raised my head above the ridgeline, machine gun fire ripped the ground all around me. I slid back down to my radioman and put in a call to the CO. I had seen where they were firing from, and I asked the CO if they could take him out with tank fire. Pretty soon they located him and the big tank gun barked. When the shell exploded, it was exactly on target. The machine gun was no more. I felt a great satisfaction in seeing the rocks and dirt fly into the air along with the machine gun. We wouldn't hear any more from him this day. One thing I couldn't figure out was why they didn't throw in the big 120 MM mortar fire. If they had, it would have been a long day.

Pretty soon I began to realize I had better check on the troops around the perimeter to see if anyone had been killed or wounded. I would be totally in the open, and I didn't relish the thought but it had to be done. The mortar fire had slowed, and

I hoped they wouldn't start firing another machine gun, so I made my move and sprinted from hole to hole until I had circled the entire perimeter. I guess it surprised them so much at my brazen act that they didn't fire a round at me. When I got back to the radioman, I told him to tell the CO that no one had been killed or wounded. I breathed a sigh of relief, but before the day was over I would make my run around the perimeter several

*Richard Uhl, center, wounded in action and shown here in a hospital in Japan.*

more times. They never did fire on me again with a machine gun. I was convinced that the tank fire had made a believer out of them.

After the initial flurry of mortar and small arms fire, it turned into a cat and mouse game that would last all day. The Chinese knew where I was, and for hours they walked mortar fire up the hill to the very edge of my fighting hole. I guess they had it in for me, and they spent the day trying to kill me. They would throw in a white smoke round in behind us and then walk the live rounds up the hill about 20 feet apart, and the last one that landed would land dangerously close to our hole. Every time they repeated the cycle it was always the third round that would explode ever so close to us. After we figured it all out, we would crawl out of the hole just before they fired the third round and thus avoid the round that was meant to kill us. This game went on for hours. Two or three times during the day a round would hit squarely in the hole where we had been. They were determined to get me. Several times they almost did.

**********

The day dragged on and the Chinese hammered us with mortar fire all day. Time after time I would check the perimeter to make sure no one was dead or wounded. They had a mortar firing from behind a small hill down in the valley that was giving us fits. I called the CO and asked for artillery fire on the mortar. He refused and told me they couldn't fire on that small a target. My temper flared, and I reminded him I was told to call in all targets that I could and especially one that was such a danger to us. "This mortar is going to kill someone lieutenant if we don't knock him off."

They still refused so I had to let it drop. I was boiling mad. If the mortar fire killed anyone, I would scream a lot when I got back to the MLR. My radioman told me if I kept on I would probably be a private when I got back. As it turned out, no one got hit, but that didn't change the principle of the thing. I was mad for a week after that, but it didn't change a thing. Later that evening, the CO finally ordered us back to the MLR.

When we got the order to leave Crete, it was getting late and it wouldn't be long until darkness would move in. I told my radioman to stay put and not to disconnect the sound power phone until the last moment. I told him that he and I would be the last to leave. For the last time that day I made the rounds of the perimeter and proceeded to send two or three men back at a time until all the platoon was cleared out. I fully expected the Chinese to hit us with mortar and machine gun fire once we left the fighting holes. It didn't happen and I breathed a sigh of relief when the last three men scrambled out of their fighting hole and headed down the back slope of Crete. Now the radioman and I were the only ones left on the ridge. I waited a few minutes until the rest of the platoon cleared the rice paddies below and began to climb the ridge that led to the top of the 2nd Platoon outpost. It was then that I told the radioman to cut the phone wire, and we headed down the back slope of Crete behind the rest of the platoon. Strangely, the Chinese didn't throw in any mortar or machine gun fire. I was still convinced the tank fire support that I had was what kept them at bay. Just before I left the ridgeline, I couldn't help but give

98

*Master Sergeant Denzil Batson, left; Corporal Kenneth Lipps, center; Sergeant Arthur Wahl, right. Near 2nd Platoon CP, east of Little Gibraltar Hill, March 1952.*

them a wave of contempt. I made a vow I would even up the score if the opportunity ever presented itself. My chance would come before long.

It had been a long and tense day, and the faces of the 2nd Platoon troops showed it. We were glad to get back, and all of us agreed we were lucky to not have had one casualty from the pounding we had taken all day. I reported to the CO that evening, and before I left I added, "Sir, we didn't dig an inch of dirt; we were too busy ducking the mortar fire."

When I got back to my Platoon CP a little later, I removed my cartridge belt and field jacket. To my amazement I discovered a couple of ragged holes just under the sleeve of my field jacket. All of a sudden I realized how close some of the machine gun bullets had come to me. Then I thought of what my old 1st sergeant had jokingly told me a lot of times. "Batson, you are so skinny they will never hit you." I had to smile, and had he still been here he would never have let me hear the last of it.

Also, I discovered two or three pieces of shrapnel stuck in my right leg. I pulled them out and the medic smeared a little iodine on the wounds, and that was the end of that. He joked with me that I ought to get the Purple Heart. Years later I would hear of all kinds of medals being handed out for less wounds than the ones I got. Other than the medic and my radio man, no one in the platoon ever knew about my close call on Crete that day. Not that it mattered one way or the other.

**********

The next day the 1st Platoon went out, and the Chinese fired on them all day. For some reason they took three or four of my 2nd Platoon troops. That night when they returned they were carrying two men, both were from my platoon. A mortar round exploded in the hole they were in and had killed Robert McCune and John Newland. I was deeply sorry to lose them, but what could I say or do that would change anything.

The very next day the 2nd Platoon would be called on again. The new officer took them out this time. When they got to the top of the hill, the Chinese were waiting for them. They had walked into an ambush. I don't want to sound like an expert, but I had warned the new officer several times that I thought the Chinese would have an ambush set up. For once I was right. In the short firefight, a few were wounded and the new officer took a grenade in the back, which blew a hole in him, as big as a silver dollar. Before the fight was over, the whole company was committed. I took a machine gun crew out to the outpost hill, but by then things had begun to settle down. We didn't stay out very long. The fight was about over, and we returned to the MLR.

When I got back to my CP, there were several wounded men standing around. Most of them were really hurting, so I took it on myself to send them all back to the aid station. I took all the names of the wounded people so the 1st sergeant could account for them on his morning report. I honestly thought I was doing the right thing, and my only reason for doing what I did was to help the 1st sergeant and the company commander. Pretty soon the company commander called me to the sound power phone, and for five minutes he chewed my rear end. He told me that I shouldn't have sent the wounded people back to the aid station until he said so, and then he told me he was the company commander and he would run the company if I didn't mind. I couldn't believe what I was hearing, and I told him I didn't have any intention of trying to run the company; all I wanted to do was help him out and get the wounded men back to the aid station. What set him off I never knew, but I told him I wouldn't send any more people back, and I didn't. The names I had written down I gave to the 1st sergeant. I made a vow then and there that I wouldn't do anything else for the company commander unless I was ordered to do so. This was all another incident that happened in Korea that made me wonder what kind of leadership we had, and another thing that prompted me to leave the military after three years. Sometimes I felt like telling them to shove the job of platoon leader up their rear and go back to just being a rifleman in one of the squads. After all, the men in the squads were the ones who won wars.

I was at the MLR when the entire 2nd Platoon made it back. The wounded officer was taken to the aid station and would never return to the company. After three days I was once again platoon leader of the 2nd Platoon. When they carried the lieutenant away, he reached out and shook my hand. The last thing he said was, "Sergeant, you were right, they were waiting for us."

What I couldn't figure out was why a master sergeant like me could see things like this ambush coming and the higher ranking officers in the company and at Battalion couldn't see past the end of their noses. Why couldn't they understand that the Chinese would be checking out what we were up to on Crete and be waiting for us? That's exactly what happened. My men and I had talked about it for three days. Now we had lost an officer and some enlisted men, all because somebody was too stupid to do his job. If some officer in the company had been smart enough to plaster the hill that morning with artillery, we could have killed a bunch of Chinese. If we had done that, it would have been the Chinese who were carrying the dead and wounded back to their line instead of us. The Chinese had gotten away without a scratch. Just two days ago I had called for artillery on a mortar that was giving us fits and was refused by the company commander, and I assume the battalion commander. Is there any wonder nobody blasted the hill that morning just in case the Chinese were there? And they were! What a botched opportunity it was. The fact that I had been talking about an ambush was totally ignored and never mentioned. I guess they figured a master sergeant didn't deserve to be given credit for calling the shots on this one. I had no doubt that my 2nd Platoon and me were not looked on too highly by the present company commander. Truth of the matter was, we were the best platoon in the company, and we proved it over and over again. I'm also sure that my job as a platoon leader was equal to anyone else in the company. At least I was smart enough to smell out an ambush. I was also smart enough not to say another word about it and let it go. I had been taught to respect an officer, and I would continue to do so.

The rest of my time in Korea I wouldn't see another officer in the platoon. One day they offered me a Battlefield Commission. I refused it, and I would return to the States a master sergeant. Being a rifle platoon leader in combat had a way of making you think twice about a career in the army.

The fact that I turned down a battlefield commission and had my differences with a few officers in the company and at Battalion didn't mean that I disliked all officers. That couldn't be further from the truth. For instance, Colonel Halverson who was my battalion CO for a while was one of the best officers I ever saw, and I had all the respect in the world for him. In addition to being a smart man, he had all the compassion in the world for the troops. Also Captain Vasgien, who would be my company commander at the end of my tour in Korea, was also a great officer. I have already mentioned Stilman Hazeltine and Ralph Robertson who were two of the best I ever saw. For all of them I had nothing but the highest praise. No doubt there were a lot of good officers, but I'll tell you here and now that we had our share of the bad ones. It is my personal opinion, but I was convinced a lot of officers in Korea were out to make one more rank, and it didn't matter how many people they walked over to make it. Most of these guys could care less about the troops in the trenches. I would say that their kind was in the minority, but nevertheless, I saw a few of them, and it made my blood boil. I had no use and no respect for them; I simply tried to avoid having any trouble with them. This is the kind of thing that influenced me to leave the Army after three years, even though I was told by a lot of high-ranking people that I had a great future in the military.

**********

After the loss of several men and the violent reaction of the Chinese, the operation on Crete was called off. Thus another round of the so-called "trench warfare" was over. The action had cost the 2nd Platoon two dead and four wounded. The other platoons lost some troopers, so "F" Company was smaller than ever and we wouldn't get any more replacements for at least two months. Also, a few casualties resulted from the bitter winter cold, such as frozen toes and fingers. As for me, the winter cold didn't seem to bother me very much. I always wore two pair of socks and regular combat boots. I never had any trouble with my feet. I wore a single set of long underwear under my fatigues and field jacket and a pair of cloth army gloves. I never came close to getting frostbite. Under my helmet I wore a wool hood to keep my ears warm, so to me the winter wasn't a problem. I firmly believed that growing up on a farm in South Missouri where I spent hours, day and night, in the cold had made me hard as nails even though I only weighed 140 pounds. I was all bone and muscle, thus my ability to take all kinds of weather. Most of the 2nd Platoon was made up of hillbillies and farmers from the Midwest, and they were tough as nails and could go all day non-stop. I wouldn't have traded them for anyone else.

It was around the time we were having all the action on Crete that the 2nd Platoon lost another one of our men. Richard Uhl who had been in the platoon for a long time was almost killed when a Chinese mortar round landed almost on top of him. He was badly wounded in the leg and wrist. He would never return to the company. I hated to see him go, but at the same time I was glad that the fight was over for him. In just three days the platoon had lost two dead and four wounded; every one of them was a combat veteran.

At this point in time I must make mention of the fact that all the men in the 2nd Platoon had been in Korea for a long time, and most of us had had our baptism of fire in combat, so we were what you would call combat veterans. All of us knew what it was to hear the death song of small arms fire

*Master Sergeant Denzil Batson and R.O.K. soldier near the 2nd Platoon CP, January 1952.*

and the exploding mortar and artillery shells. A lot of these guys had already been wounded and had returned to the platoon. We were a close-knit group, and you can't believe the friendships that developed between some of these men. They would go to hell and back for each other, and I had nothing but the highest praise for all of them. I spent a lot of time just walking down the trenchline at night and checking on everyone. These guys would be sitting around in groups just talking about anything that came to mind. I would stop and just listen to them shooting the breeze, and it was an entertaining moment for me. It wouldn't be long until the conversation would be about family and the folks back home. Pretty soon it would get quiet and the silence was deafening. You could read the homesickness in the faces of these dog face soldiers, and I knew exactly how they felt. The sad truth was, some of them would never make it back home to see the families they talked about so much. When I walked back to my platoon CP, I had to fight back the tears. I wondered how many platoon sergeants in this bloody war cared as much about their men as I did.

**********

A night or two after the fight on Crete all the platoon sergeants in the company gathered in my Platoon CP for a card game. I wasn't much interested in playing cards, so I kept the coffee hot on some little cans of gas you could light like a stove. Inside the CP we had lit a bunch of candles that lit the place up pretty good. Someone had come up with a battery radio that would pick up a radio station in Japan. While the card game went on, I sat back and listened to some country music and some gospel songs that I had heard at home a lot. Gosh! This was almost like living in a plush motel back home. Who cared if there were a million Chinese over on the next hill!

I wondered how things were going back home. At that moment I would have given anything to see my wife and family. Pretty soon an old church hymn started playing on the radio and it went something like this:

> *Precious Lord take my hand*
> *Lead me on, let me stand.*
> *I am tired, I am weak and*
> *I am worn. Through the storm*
> *Through the night*
> *Lead me on to the light,*
> *Take my hand, precious Lord*
> *Lead me home.*

Frankly, I thought the words of the song pretty well fit the troops of the 2nd Platoon.

After the card game broke up, I stretched out on a sleeping bag. Somewhere over to the east of us I could hear a machine gun chattering like a woodpecker and the explosion of an occasional artillery round. Somebody was in a fight … I went to sleep with the sound of battle ringing in my ears. That night I dreamed of my wife and my family back home. Somehow I knew I would see all of them before long.

**********

The last days of March were upon us, and my 23rd birthday had passed. The cold winter winds blew down across the 38th Parallel. Sometimes the snow would swirl across the hills and rice paddies. It put a damper on the patrol action. At night the temperature would drop to 20 degrees below zero. Any water or any kind of liquid would freeze solid. One night it began to sleet and a cold rain began to fall. It would freeze when it hit the ground. In spite of all the bad weather our routine stayed about the same. For several days no contact was made with the Chinese. It looked as if neither side wanted to start much of a fight in the bad and cruel weather.

It wasn't long before someone came up with the idea that they wanted to capture some Chinese prisoners, so every patrol we went out on for a week was planned to do just that. We were not successful, and we didn't hear of anyone else who was. It seemed as if the Chinese had completely vanished in the snow-covered hills out to our front.

One morning as a heavy fog was moving in and half of the platoon was down eating chow, a Chinese soldier walked up our safe lane like he owned the place. Before we saw him, he got within 20 yards of our trench line. Two of our men ran out and grabbed him. He didn't resist, and he didn't have any kind of weapon on him. It's a good thing he didn't run because half of the platoon had him in their sights. I called the CO from my CP and told him we had a prisoner. When he called Battalion and told them about the prisoner, you would have thought we had just captured the whole Chinese army. Some officers came up to the front in a jeep and hauled the Chinaman off to the rear. I guess he wound up in a POW camp somewhere to the south. He was a pitiful looking specimen and didn't look too bright to me. However, the officer who came up and got him acted like he was a top Chinese general.

**********

One sunny morning in early April, I got my chance to make the Chinese pay a small price that, deep down inside of me, I had been waiting to do for a long time. I was inside my CP when one of my men came in and told me I should go and take a look to our front and see what was going on. A few minutes later I was scanning the front slope of the ridgeline that ran to the

106

west of "317" with my field glasses. To my amazement a dozen people were out in plain view walking around like they were on a Sunday afternoon stroll in the park. In the next few moments I had old memories flash across my mind of all the troops that had been killed in my 2nd Platoon. It was then and there I made up my mind they were going to pay if I could pull it off. I could well remember the day on Crete when they pounded us all day with mortar fire. Now I planned to do some pounding of my own. I ran back to my CP and I asked the nearby tank commander if he could fire on the people to our front. He told me he could but would have to have clearance from the company commander before he could fire. I ran into my CP and grabbed the phone. Luckily the company commander was in the Company CP. When I told him what was going on, he quickly gave permission to fire on them. I raced back over to the tank and informed the tank commander he was cleared to open fire. I told him to kill all of them if he could. When they opened fire with the big gun, I was amazed at the accuracy that they displayed. When the first round exploded among the enemy soldiers, three or four of them went down. The others fled for the top of the ridgeline, but the big tank gun kept firing, and as far as I could tell not one of them made it. The last one to go down was trying to crawl over the ridge. Another Chinese was reaching out to help him when the big gun boomed again. Both of them disappeared over the ridge. When the tank stopped firing, a silence fell across the hills that was almost scary. I climbed up on the tank and congratulated the crew and thanked them for a great job. This was the second time I had asked them for help, and they had come through with flying colors. They could fire that big tank gun more accurately than I could fire a carbine. The next time I talked to the CO I told him that it looked like a clean sweep and that I personally didn't think any of the enemy soldiers got away.

That night I sat in my CP and tried to sort it all out. The question kept popping in my mind, why would they send a group of people out in the open like they did? Surely they must have known what our reaction would be. I guess they figured if we could send people out in broad daylight, they could do the same.

I had gotten some measure of revenge, but after it was all over it sort of left a hollow feeling in the pit of my stomach. The tank crew had done the firing, but deep down I knew I had been the instigator. Seeing people die would never appeal to me; yet the next time a situation like this arose, I knew I would react the same way. How is it that a man can kill someone and yet feel sorry for them? That's how it is in war, and that is a question that remains with you for a lifetime. That night I wrote my wife and told her how good I was having it in Korea. Truth was, I was sick of the killing and the dying.

**********

One evening the company commander stopped by my CP and asked me if I would take a small patrol back in the hills behind our lines. He wanted to see if we could flush out some North Korean infiltrators who were firing on our trucks and jeeps when they traveled the road back and forth to the MLR. He had already talked to the battalion commander, so I was elected to go the next day about noon. I left most of the platoon at the MLR and took only five or six men with me. We headed back into the hills to see what we could find. We were told to fire on anyone who looked suspicious or tried to give us any trouble. I assured the CO we would do just that. In the back of my mind I had to wonder what would happen to us if we ever got in a firefight in a village and killed a bunch of people.

The first thing we did was search out the small hills that bordered the road that led south from our frontline positions. We didn't find a thing for at least three miles so before darkness began to fall, we doubled back towards our line a little deeper into the hills and further from the road. Every now and then we would come upon a small village hidden back in the hills, and in all of them we found a few elderly men and women who apparently had come back to their home. In the rice paddies there was some evidence these elderly people were farmers and were working the land. It amazed me that they would be trying to farm this close to the front line. As we walked through the small villages, the elderly Koreans would stand and stare at us as we walked by. Every time we passed through one of these small villages, I had the chilling feeling that other eyes beside the farmers were watching us as we went by. Frankly, I was suspicious of any Korean who stayed close to the frontline. I didn't trust any of these civilians.

When darkness began to fall, we were still about three miles in back of our line. We had all pretty well decided it was like trying to find a "needle in a haystack" to find the people who were shooting at our trucks and jeeps. All the North Koreans had to do was just blend into the civilian population when we showed up. It was a frustrating thing to try and find them. They just had too many places to hide and, to us, they all looked alike. A couple of the troopers told me they figured the only way to cure the problem was to just shoot everyone in the village.

Total darkness had fallen now, but a bright moon was out and lit up the area. Back to the east was a small village that couldn't have been over three miles from the frontline. I decided to check it out before we called it a day. When we approached, you could see a fairly large group of Koreans gathered under a straw-roofed hut that was open on three sides. All of a sudden they began to sing a song that sounded like "Amazing Grace." I realized we had walked up on a church service in progress. Pretty soon they stopped singing, and a man who looked like an American walked over to me and asked what we wanted and if there was any problem. I couldn't believe what I had just seen — a church service being held this close to the frontline. I told him what we were doing and that I wasn't aware he was holding a church service when we walked up. He told me he was from the eastern United States and he had been here for several years and that he quite often held church services this close to the frontline.

I asked him if he realized he was within easy range of the communist's mortar and artillery fire. He said he did and he still planned to hold church services and (wouldn't you know it?) he invited me to come. I had to decline the invitation, but I couldn't help but admire the courage of this man. I shook his hand and wished him well. When we walked away and headed for our line, I still had the creepy feeling North Korean eyes were watching us.

An hour later we were back to our line and reported no contact to the CO. The next few days, however, there was no more firing on our vehicles. That made me believe that the

American preacher had some snakes attending his church service. I wanted to go back, but the CO said no.

* * * * * * * * * *

The first week of April came to a close, and this was the beginning of my fourth month in a row on the frontline. In the seven months that I had been in Korea, almost six of them had been spent up front. A lot had happened to us, and we began to wonder if we would ever get a break. The constant strain and pressure that is on a frontline soldier is beyond explanation. The many patrols and the constant danger began to take its toll on everybody. I had forgot what it was to relax, even for a moment. At night when you tried to sleep, you slept with one eye open. When it rained and you got wet, you dried out from your body heat. There weren't any warm fires to stand around or houses to get into on the frontline in Korea. Sometimes inside your bunker, the rats would run around like they owned the place. If one of them bit you, it would usually mean a high fever that could kill you. When the weather begins to warm, the mud would get six inches deep in the bunkers and the trenches. We had forgotten what it was to have a bath or a clean change of clothes. If we shaved, it was with filthy rice paddy water. In addition to all of that, the dead Chinese bodies and the rice paddies began to stink so badly it was unbelievable. Despite all this, we would eat chow as if the air was pure as fresh flowers. A lot of the new guys couldn't eat chow with all the stink, and they would look at us like we were crazy. However, after a while and after they got hungry enough, they would eat just like the rest of us.

One day they sent a bunch of men from Regiment up to our area to clear out all the dead Chinese that were lying around. By the time they had cleared them all out and loaded them on a truck to haul them away, the whole crew was so drunk they couldn't drive the truck. I never did know how it all came out. We laughed for a week about it. To all of us they put on the best show we had seen while in Korea. Where they got the booze to get drunk was a mystery to us.

**********

It was still the early part of April when the company commander stopped in my Platoon CP one afternoon. I could tell he had something on his mind. It didn't take him long to let me in on what he was thinking.

"Sergeant, I'm going to try something different than what we have been doing in the past. Instead of sending out platoon and squad-size patrols, I want to try sending out just one man with a 'walkie-talkie' radio and field glasses. I

*William Ray and Ron Stewart, standing in front of 2nd Platoon tent, North Kimpo in Korea.*

want to see if we can locate and call in targets for our artillery and maybe our tanks to fire on. Whoever goes out will have to get in a good position before daylight and try to keep from being seen while observing the activity that might be going on. If, in fact, we can keep from being seen we might be able to hit them with artillery or tank fire when they don't expect it. I'll tell the other platoons what I have in mind, and I'll let you know later who I'll call on to do the job. I don't know how effective it will be, but I intend to give it a try." Then he asked me what I thought about it. I told him I felt the same way he did and that was to give it a try and see what happened. What else could I tell my company commander? With that, he left for the Company CP. A little later that evening he called me and said to get someone ready to go out. He told me he thought it should be a squad leader or anyone who was capable of calling in artillery fire. I told him I would get someone to volunteer and I would get back with him shortly.

For the next hour I mulled over in my mind who I would send out on this one-man patrol. Two of my squad leaders said they would go, but after I thought about it for a while I decided I would go myself. It would be the first and last time I would volunteer for anything while in Korea. Later that evening I

111

went up to the Company CP and told the CO I was going to go out myself. We went over all the plans, and I pointed out to him on the map where I intended to go. He agreed and wished me luck. He assured me they would be standing by if I called in any enemy targets. The place I had decided to go was on the back slope of the ridgeline Crete. I had been there several times, and I knew of a spot where I felt like I could pretty well hide and at the same time be able to observe the enemy. I would be closer to their MLR than ours. Outside of all the obvious dangers, the thing that worried me the most was the "walkie-talkie" radio I would be carrying. They were famous for not working when you needed them the most. This day would be no different.

Before daylight the next morning I was on my way out to Crete. At the moment I had two other men with me, but once we got to my destination they would leave me and go back to the MLR. Once we cleared our safe lane, instead of going over the top of the 2nd Platoon outpost, we skirted it to the right and headed directly across the rice paddies to the base of Crete. The moon was out, so it was easy to see where we were going. At the moment I was worried about who might be on our 2nd Platoon outpost as it would be behind me and between the MLR and me. The men of the 2nd Platoon who had been on the outpost all night had already gone back to the company area. That in itself was enough to make me wonder why I had volunteered for this patrol.

When we reached the top of the ridge, we crawled over the ridgeline instead of walking so as not to be seen on the skyline. About 30 yards away was my destination, so the two men who were with me departed for our MLR. Once I was alone and hidden in my hiding place, I began to wonder what I had gotten myself into. Every fear that you could think of crept into my mind. I had to fight off the panic and try to stay calm. Daylight finally came, and I could see clearly the rice paddies and small hills that lay out to my front. At the moment there wasn't a sign of any movement of any kind. For the next hour I scanned the ridges with my field glasses, but nothing happened. It was so quiet you could hear a pin drop. I looked back behind me to the top of the ridge; I knew I was vulnerable from behind. Someone could come in from that direction, and if they did it would be a long day. I finally decided to try my radio and see if it would work; it didn't. Now I was really in a pickle. If I needed to call for artillery fire, I couldn't, and that would put an end to what we were trying to do. I pressed the button on the radio and tried to call again. It still wouldn't work. Now it was decision time, and I tried to decide what to do. Without any way to reach anyone, it would do no good to stay here.

At that moment the Chinese decided the issue for me. A mortar round slammed in and exploded in the rocks about 20 feet below me. If I didn't move, I knew the next one would come in on me. I leaped to my feet and raced for the top of the ridge. Another round came in and exploded in the rocks where I had been. I reached the top of Crete and headed down the back slope to the rice paddies below. Once across the rice paddies I reached the corner of our 2nd Platoon outpost. It was then and only then I began to relax. I tried my radio again, and this time I got the CO. I reported to him what had happened, and he told me I had made the right decision and to return to the MLR.

In the next few days a couple more people went out with about the same results. The Chinese were on to what we were doing, so the one-man patrol operation was halted. The "walkie-talkie" radio had failed the others just like it did me, but the truth was we had all been spotted by the Chinese, and that put a damper on what we were trying to do anyway.

**********

Along in the middle of April, I got the chance to climb the back slope of Little Gibraltar Hill again. The Company CO called me to the Company CP and gave me the details on a patrol that night. We were to set up an ambush down on the front slope of Little Gibraltar directly in front of "E" Company's positions. Instead of going out the safe lane, he told me we would go down the road behind Little Gibraltar, climb the hill, and go through "E" Company's position. We would then proceed down the front slope to our ambush site. A little enemy activity had been reported over here, giving us a reason for the ambush.

That night the moon was out and it was light as day. We moved down the road behind "E" Company and prepared to climb the hill. I stopped for a moment and looked around. Old

113

memories began to flood my mind. Just over to my left were the bunkers we had used to get in just before the assault in November. To the right I could see the path leading up the side of the hill where the Chinese had plastered us with mortar fire when we were trying to get back to the top to help "E" Company. But tonight we were going up the hill for a different reason.

As we began to climb, we passed the spot where my old buddy Sergeant Brandanger had been killed. It seemed like a long time ago since that had happened. Pretty soon we reached the top and across the little valley and in front of me lay old familiar Peak III where I had spent one of the darkest days of my life. When we got on top of Peak III, I stopped again and looked around for a moment. All the old familiar spots where I had spent a long and awful day were still here. I had a strange feeling at this moment that I would never be here again. I just stood for a few seconds and remembered that terrible day — then we moved on down the slope. We set up our ambush at the bottom of the hill. We stayed all night and nothing happened. Early in the morning we came back through "E" Company on our way back to our own position. I was bringing up the rear of the Platoon; just when we cleared "E" Company, I heard one of the trooper's remarks, "Those guys have probably never seen a bit of combat." I stopped again and remembered all the awful times we had on this rock pile. I turned and took one more look at Peak III. I would never see it again. We then headed on down the hill. This hill and all that had happened here would be branded across my soul for the rest of my life.

**********

Late one evening I was sitting in the Platoon CP getting a list of all the men in the platoon together to take up to the Company CP for the 1st Sergeant and the company commander. It was a continuous job for the 1st sergeant to keep his morning reports in order and correct. All the other platoons were turning in a platoon roster the same as I was. When I started to leave the CP, I almost ran into a lieutenant who was one of the officers at Battalion. On the road behind him were about 15 Koreans carrying picks and shovels. All of them were dressed in quilted uniforms, sort of Chinese style, and they all squatted Korean style at the side of the road.

When I asked the Lieutenant what was going on, he told me he needed my help. He told me, "When it gets dark I have to take these Korean laborers out near Crete in no man's land and leave them with some people to do some digging on some bunkers and trenches. These Koreans are supposed to be protected while they work. Once we get them out to where they are supposed to go, we leave and come back. Sarge, I need your help to take them out and, frankly, I don't know of anyone who knows the place out there like you do."

When I didn't say anything for a moment, he continued. "Sergeant, I know what you are thinking, and it sounds just as stupid to me as it does to you, but I still need your help." The lieutenant was a friend of mine, and I knew I couldn't do anything but help him out. At one time he had almost become my platoon leader, but Battalion decided they needed him.

I said, "Lieutenant, I'll do it, but let me tell you I don't like it one bit. We could run into Chinese out there. If we do, the two of us could be in for a long night. Come to think of it — it could be a short night. It makes no difference — you would order me to go anyway, wouldn't you?"

His response, "Sarge, you guessed it." So that settled it.

I took a pair of field glasses, and along with the lieutenant I went over to the 3rd Platoon area so I could better see where we were going. I soon discovered where we would take this bunch of civilians. I told the lieutenant I hoped the Chinese wouldn't be on the prowl tonight. All we could do was hope we didn't run into trouble.

We would go out our safe lane and turn right or northeast and go all the way to the east end of Crete to a small hill that was where the other people were supposed to wait for us. Getting there was no problem for me, but I told the Lieutenant, "Just in case we run into trouble, stay close to me because there are mine fields out there. I know where they are and you don't."

He replied, "Just exactly why I asked you to go."

When we got back to my CP the Koreans were still squatting at the place we had left them. The lieutenant pointed out the Korean who was supposed to sort of be the leader of the group. He also informed me that he was a North Korean and so were some of the others. He remarked that he hoped they didn't try to defect back north, now that they were this close to the Chinese and North Korean line. "You can't trust these people anywhere." He said.

I had been on the frontline for a long time, and my fuse was pretty short. When the lieutenant had told me all this stuff about the Koreans, he put the match to the fuse. I walked over to the leader of the bunch and told him to get up. When we got nose to nose, I asked him if he could understand English. He said he could, so I told him to "Listen up — and pass this on to all your friends. I don't like any North Korean, and when we go out tonight, I want you and your friends to know that if you try to run out on us, I'll blow your brains out with this carbine. If that's not enough, I'll stick this bayonet clear through you. Another thing, when we leave you out there, don't try to sneak out and come back through our safe lane. If you do, my platoon will kill you. That leaves you two choices — either stay out there and work or head north."

The Korean lost his smile and turned to tell his friends what I had said. I had gotten my point across. From then on I wasn't very popular with the Koreans. I could care less what

*M / Sgt. William H. Drummond, Platoon Sgt., 3rd Platoon, and lead scout on the attack at Little Gibralatar Hill*

they thought. The lieutenant asked me later if I meant what I said. I did.

A big bright Chinese moon hung in the sky when we left the 2nd Platoon trench line. I was in front of the column, and the lieutenant was bringing up the rear. That way we had these birds covered from both ends. We followed the 2nd Platoon safe lane out to the foot of our outpost and then turned northeast toward Crete. It was a good quarter-mile to where we were going. The company commander had told me he would have people ready if we got into trouble. It was a help to know that, but the hair still crawled on the back of my neck. I hoped and prayed we wouldn't run into an American patrol. The quilted uniforms the Koreans wore looked just like the Chinese in the moonlight. The very thought of it scared me to death. I could just see some GI sighting in a BAR on this bunch, and I was in front.

It was slow but we finally got to our destination. The people who were there took over the Koreans, and the lieutenant and I were free to go. We didn't waste any time heading back the way we had come. We made good time back to the 2nd Platoon outpost and turned left and entered our safe lane. A little later we were back at the 2nd Platoon CP. The lieutenant thanked me and left for Battalion. I told my platoon medic that if anyone had fired on the Koreans and they ran into the rice paddies, the land mines would still be exploding. Lord, I was glad that didn't happen.

I never did find out how the project with the Korean civilians came out. But had the Chinese hit them that night, it would have been a slaughter. It totally amazed me why and how anyone could come up with a brainstorm like that. I stayed up all night fully expecting to have to go pull them out of the fire, but luckily the Chinese didn't happen to discover what was going on. If trouble had started I would, for sure, have had to commit the whole platoon. I breathed a big sigh of relief when nothing happened. The lieutenant from Battalion who helped me take out the Koreans that night said the Korean leader, who I gave my little speech, said I was crazy.

**********

If you think there was always unity in "F" Company, think again. At this time during our stay at Little Gibraltar Hill we had a captain who was our company commander, and from day one I didn't like anything about him. I had clashed with him several times and, frankly, I just didn't have any confidence in his leadership. I was used to being around officers like Stilman Hazeltine, my former company commander, who was one of the best. Also Lieutenant Robertson, who was the best platoon leader I ever seen. Then, of course, a few others like Lieutenant Joe Pullian, Lieutenant Warden and Lieutenant Nicoli who had been killed a few weeks ago at the Imjin River. In my opinion, all these men were great responsible officers that I had a lot of confidence in. Now, of course, they were all gone. At this point in time the platoon sergeants in "F" Company were doing the job of platoon leaders in place of an officer. I was one of them.

This one particular evening about dark a jeep pulled up to my Platoon CP and stopped. It was the captain, and with him were the 1st sergeant and two other sergeants from the 1st and 3rd Platoons. They informed me they were going back to the kitchen tents about two miles down the road and throw a beer party that night. When I asked who was in charge while they were gone, I was told I was. They told me if I needed any help they could be contacted at the cook's tent back in the rear. For a while I thought they were kidding; then I realized that they, in fact, were not. When they left, all of a sudden I found myself the ranking man in "F" Company. A thousand fears crept into my mind, and I hoped the Chinese wouldn't choose this night to attack. The first thing I did was get in contact with all the other platoons to make sure I could get in touch with them later if I needed to. I had my radioman with me in the Platoon CP so I could call for artillery if I had to. I was so keyed up, I spent all night contacting all the squads and the other platoon. They probably thought I was crazy.

Standing in a fighting hole next to the Platoon CP with my radioman, I had time to mull over in my mind the situation I was in. Lord! What an awesome responsibility I was in! I decided then and there I would never be an officer in the army. I didn't sleep a wink all night. Deep down I was steaming with anger because all the leaders were gone to the rear. When daylight finally came, I breathed a sigh of relief. After a while the CO and the others made it back. I tried not to let my anger show, but I would have enjoyed choking every one of them. I didn't mind them having a beer party, but I resented being left with the company and the awesome responsibility that scared me to death. The day this captain left the company was good news to me. I guess I was a spoiled brat, but I couldn't agree with anything he did while he was with "F" Company.

**********

The last patrol I went out on at Little Gibraltar Hill would be the longest and the most frustrating operation I had ever been on. They sent a truck up to the MLR, and we loaded up and were transported about three or four miles to the east to another battalion area that was located near a place called "Outpost Kelly" and another hill called "Cavite." It was here we de-trucked and waited for darkness to fall before moving out. This was supposed to be a "contact patrol," which simply meant between here and our positions back at Little Gibraltar Hill we were supposed to seek out the enemy and engage him in a firefight. We were supposed to sweep the valley that extended from here all the way back to Crete and Little Gibraltar Hill. We would do this, and it would be a long and frustrating night.

When darkness fell across the hills, we headed down into the valley near Outpost Kelly. I was sure that here was where we would make contact, but it didn't happen. As the night dragged on, we hit every small hill and all the rice paddies in the valley, but to no avail. It seemed as if the Chinese had completely vanished. There wasn't a sign of the Chinese anywhere. When we reached the east end of Crete, I called the company commander and told him our situation. We were told to continue on down the ridgeline all the way to the west end of Crete and call him back if we ran into trouble. We would do this, and still no contact was made with the enemy. This time I called the company commander and asked what he wanted us to do. Shortly he told me to return to the MLR. As bad as they wanted to make contact with the enemy, I was surprised we were ordered back to the company area. The only thing that I could see for us to do was assault the Chinese MLR, and that would have been suicide.

All the way back to our positions I had time to ponder this operation. As for me, I was convinced the whole operation stunk. For the first time in Korea I seriously questioned the purpose of a patrol. Why would we be hauled three or four miles away to go out on this operation? It didn't make any sense to me, and I wondered who had dreamed this one up. If the enemy was active over near another Battalion, why were they not sent out to take care of the problem that was in their area? By the time we got back to our trench-line, I was seething with anger. As for as I was concerned, some officer was trying to feather his nest at the expense of the 2nd Platoon. It was a personal opinion, but I had no doubt I was right. In all my time in Korea I always tried to value a man's life, and when I saw someone who didn't care and would sacrifice men's lives for no reason other than to make himself look good, it made my blood boil. It burned me up to think that we actually had men in the army who could care less about other people's lives. It was nice to know that not very many of that kind were around. However, one was enough.

Prior to us returning to the MLR and out of pure frustration, I told all the guys to point their weapons at the ridgeline that ran up to the top of "317" and blast off a few rounds. We did this and then headed for home. All night long up in that area some "Chink" had been firing a "burp-gun." I hoped we lucked out and nailed him. After we fired in his direction, the "burp-gun stopped firing. I figured we either hit him or scared him to death.

Let me say here and now that the frustration I felt on my last patrol at Little Gibraltar had been with me for a long time. I kept all my differences of opinion to myself, but sometimes I had my doubts about the smarts of the people who planned all our patrols. Some of them made sense, but most of them didn't. A few times I had made a few mild protests about certain patrols, but in spite of how I saw it we went out and did the best we could. At no time did we disobey an order, even though sometimes the things we were asked to do and the places we were asked to go were totally unreasonable and, yes, almost impossible. A few times we were sent out so close to the Chinese MLR that it was a miracle we were not totally overrun and wiped out, and for what reason? No one that I know could answer that question. Personally, I felt like that manning the screens of outposts that fronted the MLR was the most important thing we could do. The people who were on these outposts could warn the MLR of any attack that might be coming, and to me that was a positive thing to be doing that I agreed with totally. Matter of fact, one night I myself discovered Chinese troops on the prowl near our own 2nd Platoon outpost. I warned the MLR of that fact, and even though no attack came, we were ready if it had. That all makes sense to me, and not the half-hearted, spur-of-the-moment patrols that got a bunch of people killed for no reason.

After I related all my frustrations to some of the 2nd Platoon troops and said how I thought things ought to be, one of them told me, "Sarge, it just don't look like they are going to let you run this war." Talk about being put in your place! I had some men in the 2nd Platoon who told it like it really was.

**********

One warm late April night just before we were to be relieved by the British, the company commander called me from the company C.P. and informed me that the coming night we would be on 100% alert until further notice. "Sergeant, I want you to inform all the men in your platoon of what is going on and let them know that no one will be sleeping tonight. We have reports from regiment of a possible attack by the Chinese in this area, so we must take it serious and be ready if they do attack. Be sure everyone has lots of ammo and grenades, and I want you to be out among the men and see to it that all I have said is carried out. This is a very serious alert, so impress on everyone to be ready just in case. Is that all clear to you?"

"Yes, sir! I'll get on it right now and I'll see to it that the 2nd Platoon will be ready. We already have a lot of ammo and grenades in each fighting hole, but I'll double check and make sure we have enough."

His reply, "Good, I'll inform all the other platoons and, by the way, Sergeant, don't send a squad out to the O.P. but keep them back at the line."

"Yes, sir! I'll do that. I'm going down right now and get everyone alerted."

In the next 20 minutes I had alerted every man on the line in my platoon, and as far as I was concerned we were as ready as we could get. I noticed that all the troops were taking it seriously, and most of them were putting hand grenades and ammo in a handy place where they could get to them easily. When I walked down the line about dark to see how everyone was doing, no one was saying a word. You could see all the tenseness in the faces of the troops, and I was a bundle of nerves as was always the case during these times. I found a hole to get into in the middle of the platoon perimeter, and the long night began. A couple of times I walked down the line to check on everyone. When I walked by my machine gun crew, one of them said, "Sarge, you are going to get shot running around here like you are."

I had to agree so I returned to my fighting hole. Out to our front in the rice paddies at this time in late April the frogs and the insects were hollering and singing a chorus that was deafening. The thought crossed my mind that as long as the insects were hollering that meant no Chinese were around. If, in fact, they all of a sudden stopped, that would mean someone was around. A pale moon was out and lit up the rice paddies with a pale light. It was a tense night to say the least as these alerts always were. About the time I began to relax a little, a stillness fell across the rice paddies and you could have heard a pin drop. The insects and frogs all quit hollering all at once, and I was sure this was it. In the stillness I heard some trooper mutter, "Come and get it, you slant-eyed rascals." That's exactly the way I felt. We had two machine guns, two BAR's, all with all of the other weapons on line, and we could have really made them pay a price. We were all hoping they would attack; if they had they would have paid dearly.

The night dragged on, and we stayed awake all night. When daylight finally broke, we realized that another alert turned into a false alarm. Nevertheless, we did what we should have done and we would do it again if we had to. The company commander called me later and told me that the alert was over. All the men got some sleep that day, but I didn't get to sleep a wink. By the time the next night rolled around I was so sleepy I could hardly walk around. Times like this made me wonder why I had ever become a platoon sergeant. When I complained about it to some of my men, one of them said, "Sarge, didn't you enlist in the army?"

Once again the troops pretty well put me in my place. I couldn't argue with what he said.

The warm spring winds of late April were blowing across the hills of Korea. The flowers on the hills had begun to bloom, adding a little bit of color to the countryside. The face of Korea had begun to change with the melting of the snow and ice. Instead of a dead and brown look, the hills began to turn green. The 2nd Platoon was still in the bunkers and trenches near Little Gibraltar Hill. It had been a long and cold winter and the routine continued, but it was soon to change and we would be leaving this place very soon.

One morning all the platoon leaders were told to report to the Company CP. The company commander told us to get ready to move out the following day. The British would replace us. I passed the word on to the 2nd Platoon, and everyone began to get ready to leave. Late that evening I was told to leave someone in charge of the 2nd Platoon and be ready, along with the other platoon sergeants, to ride a helicopter to our next destination. We were to relieve the Marines on the extreme north part of Kimpo Island north of the city of Seoul and across the Han River. I had mixed emotions about this move. It didn't look like we would get any reserve time. In spite of that, I was glad to be leaving Little Gibraltar Hill.

Riding the helicopter across Korea was a lot different than riding trucks along the muddy roads. I began to relax for the first time in months. It was then that I realized just how totally exhausted I really was. I leaned back against the wall of the helicopter and in a few seconds I was sound asleep.

The rest of the company would join us in a few days. After awhile we landed in an area with several big tents scattered around the place. The helicopter door opened, and we stepped out onto the ground and into the middle of a group of United States Marines. All these Marines were clean and as sharp as they could be. They looked at us like we were a bunch of misfits from the nearest stockade. Frankly, I could care less what the Marines or anyone else thought about me. I knew where we had been. It had been a long, tough four months. I doubt they could have done any better than we did.

**********

The winter at Little Gibraltar had been a long and cold four months. The number of casualties and rotations had again changed the face of the 2nd Platoon. At the time we left Little Gibraltar Hill we were down to 18 men. This was the lowest number since the battle for the hill back in November. Even though I was now one of the oldest veterans in the company, rotation seemed like a long way away to me. I tried not to think about it, but in the back of my mind I hoped the day would come soon. However, I wasn't holding my breath. The comforts of home and family in the United States at the moment seemed like just a pleasant memory and a long way down the road.

The Marines pulled out of the position on North Kimpo Island, and we moved in and took over. We didn't know it now, but our time here wouldn't be very long. This was the most unusual place we had ever been. As far as we were concerned, this place was a Sunday School picnic compared to where we had been. When the platoon arrived and I told them this was the front line, they all had a big laugh out of it. I had to laugh with them.

The month of May began a lot different than the last four months. But it would end with a flurry of activity that none of us was ready for.

# CHAPTER 5

# Kimpo Island

AFTER THE MARINES PULLED OUT of the North Kimpo Island area, we moved in and set up shop. What surprised us all was, instead of bunkers and fighting holes like we were used to being in, we moved into large platoon-size tents with bunks to sleep on, and we even had a small pot-bellied stove in the middle of the tent that burned fuel oil. This would sort of heat up the place when the nights were cold. However, warm weather was moving in fast, so we used the stove more to heat coffee than anything else. For sure, none of us had any complaints to make about our new, so-called positions. As a matter of fact, after the past seven months I felt like I was living in a fine motel. So did the others who had been living like moles in the ground on the frontline at Little Gibraltar Hill. We were served hot chow every day, and being able to eat without fear of the mortar rounds landing on or near you was great for a change. The best thing that happened was we got a clean change of clothes and a shower, which we hadn't had in months. Gosh! We felt like human beings again, and a lot of the old fire returned to the troops of the 2nd Platoon.

The big tents we were living in were dug into the backside of a ridgeline that ringed the northern-most part of the Island. At the top of the ridge the ground began a gradual slope down to the edge of a body of water that bordered on three sides of our position. To the east was the Han River that gradually gave way to the Yellow Sea, which was to our front and to our left. In this particular spot it wasn't very far across the water to where the Chinese were located. If the Chinese attacked us here, it would have to be pulled off by coming across the water, and most of us figured that wasn't very likely to happen.

However, you couldn't take anything for granted, so we stayed ready at all times. The one thing I couldn't figure out was why the Chinese didn't throw in mortar and artillery fire. In all the time we spent here the only mortar rounds I heard landed on the front slope of the ridge, and that didn't happen very often.

While here, Master Sergeant Drummond, the 3rd Platoon Sergeant, became the 1st Sergeant of "F" Company. We got a new company commander, my fourth since being in Korea. He was a captain, and other than Stilman Hazeltine, who was CO when I first arrived, Captain Vosgien was the best CO I had while I was in Korea. He was one cool customer, and I had all the respect in the world for him.

The first week passed, and about all we did was regroup and get in a few more new people and assign each of them to a Platoon. For some reason the 2nd Platoon didn't get a single replacement, so our number stayed the same, consisting of 18 men. We were way under strength, but the other Platoons had several more men than we did so as a whole "F" Company was about three-fourths strength.

**********

One day I went on patrol with three other men back in the countryside to the south of our company area. We were to check out the area and familiarize ourselves with the new location. To me, this was a good idea, as I always liked to learn a new place as soon as possible. The unusual thing about this patrol was that we rode around the back roads by jeep. All the small villages we went through were typical straw huts and dirt streets, and always present were small children who seemed to be everywhere.

At this one particular village we stopped under a small shade tree to take a break. As usual, kids come out to see us and started asking for candy or anything else they could get. While a couple of men handed out gum and candy to the kids, I took a short walk down the street near some straw huts. I rounded a corner and walked smack dab into a Korean carrying a "burp gun." I stopped, and we stared at one another for a second and neither of us made a move. Pretty soon someone in one of the nearby shacks yelled something in Korean, and the "gun-toting" Korean spun around and disappeared into one of the straw huts. In my mind I was sure this guy was a North Korean. The hatred I could see in his eyes was enough to make me believe that. I hesitated and for a moment I considered going after him, but with civilians all around me my better judgement took over, so I sort of backed around the corner and back to our jeep. I told the driver to get going. Down the road a ways I related what I had seen. The jeep driver and the other two people hadn't been in Korea very long and, frankly, I didn't know how they would react in a firefight. If I had had some of my 2nd Platoon along, it would have been "a hot time in the old town tonight." I can tell you for sure "no one" would wave a burp gun in their faces but one time. That's the difference in men who are combat veterans and others who are not.

When I got back to the company, I told Captain Vosgien about it, but it didn't cause much of a stir because nothing was ever done about it. To this day I swear I had almost walked into a Communist meeting and the man with the "burp gun" was standing guard. With only three other men with me, it wouldn't have been very smart to start anything, and besides, there were too many women and children around. A firefight in a village could have been bad for all concerned. Besides, I couldn't be all that positive about the man with the "burp gun." I'm glad it turned out the way it did, but I still had the gut feeling that I almost walked into a commie party meeting. One of the most frustrating things about Korea was when something like this happened no one wanted to believe you.

The next day I went out on another patrol, only this time we walked and I had the whole 2nd Platoon with me. We swept the whole area and didn't run into any hostile people. However, on the way back to the Company area, we walked close by the village where I had seen the "gun-toting guy." Wouldn't you know it? A Korean man came out waving his arms and cussed us out. Most of his abuse was directed at me. One of the R.O.K soldiers in the platoon told me the guy was the mayor of the village and he was screaming at us to get out and never come back. What set him off I'll never know, but I suspected some marines or soldiers had been here before. That night back in our tent the men in the platoon told me I should take some time and polish my image with the civilians at Kimpo

Island. I told Captain Vosgien we ought to take the whole company in and clean the snakes out of the villages. He looked at me for a moment and didn't answer.

**********

The second week on Kimpo was coming to a close when I got the word my old buddy, Master Sergeant Drummond, was going home to America because of the death of his mother. He came over to my tent to say good-bye just like all the others who had gone home before. I wished him well, and after talking for awhile he left the area. When he was gone, I all of a sudden realized I was the last one of a group of 30 that had joined "F" Company in October of last year. That night I couldn't sleep a wink because of the departure of Drummond. In the past two months I had seen a lot of the old "F" Company troopers leave, and I missed every one of them very much. I had been here now for about eight months, and in a couple more months I had high hopes of leaving this place, too. That two months would seem like two years before it was over for me.

Along toward the end of May life on Kimpo had become a complete bore for the 2nd Platoon. All of us were finding it difficult to unwind from the rigors of what we called the real frontline. Life here was a Sunday School picnic compared to all we had seen in the past several months. My fear was that we would get soft and lose the sharp edge we had when we left Little Gibraltar Hill.

One night in late May I lay on my bunk and couldn't sleep a wink. Across the Han River on the mainland I could hear our big artillery guns firing a salvo. Somewhere in those dark hills someone was having a real fight with the enemy. I got up and walked outside. Across the Han River you could see the flash of the big guns against the night sky. I had seen first-hand many times what the big guns could do to a man. I wondered how many would fall this night. A couple of troopers came out and joined me. One of them asked me if I was homesick for the frontlines. I had to laugh, and I remarked I was more homesick for my wife and home than anything else. In a few days we would be leaving this place, and all of us would be having second thoughts about the easy life we were having here. Once again the 2nd Battalion would be called on to plug the gap; this time it would be at a big hill on the central front that was called "Old Baldy Hill." The 45th Infantry Division was in trouble and might need our help. Our stay at Kimpo Island was over. It had been an easy two or three weeks, but deep down I was glad to be on the move again. Does combat get in your blood? Sometimes I think it did.

**********

Our stay at Kimpo Island was a complete bore to me. Outside of a few patrols we found it difficult to pass the time away. As far as I was concerned, the patrol action was a complete joke. I was convinced that all it amounted to was to keep us from getting lazy and rusty, which wasn't a bad idea. The days we spent here did, however, give us all much needed rest. The first patrol I went out on was by jeep and actually behind our line. When the CO told me about it, I thought he was joking. To me, the so-called patrol was a pleasant ride in the countryside. What a difference compared to Little Gibraltar Hill when going on a patrol was dangerous business.

Finally, the day came when the trucks rolled up and we loaded up and headed down the road south to the Han River Bridge in the Capitol City of Seoul. Our destination was to the east of the Little Gibraltar Hill area to a place called Old Baldy Hill. From the way the company commander described it, we could be in for a rough time if we were committed. All of a sudden I decided I would have rather spent another month on Kimpo than where we were headed, as if I had any choice in the matter. Funny thing was, once you got back to the frontline you started praying to get out again.

It was a cloudy and cool day. It looked like it would start raining at any moment as we rolled down the road. I had to wonder what lay in store for us in the coming days. We would find out shortly.

Before we reached the Han River bridge to cross over into the city of Seoul, I had time to ponder the four or five months we had spent on line at Little Gibraltar Hill and on Kimpo Island the past month. If the so-called trench warfare meant that men would die for nothing, then I for one was sick of it. At Little Gibraltar we had lost dozens of good men, and for what reason? As far as I knew, we hadn't taken an inch of ground from the Chinese; yet our casualties were sky high with nothing to show for it. All across the Korean battle front it was the same story for all units on line. When I told my truck driver how frustrating it was to fight over hills that had no particular meaning except to get people killed, he agreed with me. Pure and simple, most G.I.s in Korea wanted to fight to win, I know I did. I could well remember what General Douglas MacArthur said, and it follows:

> *"Once war is forced upon us, there is no alternative than to apply every available means to bring it to a swift end. War's very object is victory, not prolonged indecision. In war there is no substitute for victory."*
>
> *General Douglas MacArthur*

To that I give a hearty "Amen."

\*\*\*\*\*\*\*\*\*\*

I would be remiss if I didn't mention the combat engineers. If you think that all they did was build roads and bridges, then think again. Here is one man's story who was with the 1092 Engineer Battalion:

### S/Sgt. James Hon

*I was drafted November 18, 1950, and inducted into the army at Chicago, Illinois. Along with other men, I was sent to Ft. Leonard Wood, Missouri, for basic training. What a surprise — when we arrived we were yelled at all day long and told how dumb and sloppy we were.*

*We began training with all types of weapons, such as grenades, machine guns, mortar and rifle. This was all very good. However, no one got any specialized training, which I feel would have been very helpful on many occasions, such as rifles with scopes, compass and map reading, also mortar and bazookas.*

*Basic training consisted of 14 weeks for my group at Ft. Leonard Wood before we shipped to Korea.*

*I was a trained diesel engine mechanic before entering the military, and when I was processed in Japan for assignment in Korea, I was sent to the Combat Engineers which had a lot of diesel-powered equipment. The people I trained with were* transported to Korea by plane and ship. The ships took 14 days and the planes about 12 hours. A lot of my group was killed before I got to Korea. I arrived at Pusan, and the smell of human waste was bad and the food was worse ... what a place. I was not very optimistic about surviving.

I arrived at my unit, located approximately 20 miles south of Seoul, called Suwon. We were greeted by the company commander who explained we were to go into a blocking position. The Chinese were trying to break through to our right. After we ate and received ammo and hand grenades, we were put in trucks and moved about four miles up a hill and unloaded. We climbed the hill for about 30 minutes to reach the top. We dug in for a long night. The artillery pounded away off and on. Several B-29 bombers started dropping bombs near Seoul, and there were a lot of flashing lights all night.

The second night we were back at the same place, and we started getting machine gun and mortar fire. Three P-51s with napalm flew past us to drop napalm on the hill facing us. One bomb was turned loose too soon and killed two of our people and wounded four or five. We had a lot of angry people. After four nights, we returned to our camp and did not go on line again.

We stayed at Suwon about one month and then moved north to Ui Jong Bu. The cold rains came down, and the dirt roads became muddy and slick. We finally arrived at the new location and set up camp. Three of us were sent back near Seoul to retrieve a trailer someone had lost. As we were traveling south about 8 p.m., a sniper shot the man in the back who was sitting next to me. We put him in a Canadian ambulance which was just behind us, and he was transported to a Mash hospital. The man survived and was sent home. After he was shot, I grabbed my M-1 rifle and went out across a field to a small hill where I knew the sniper had been, but the sniper got away. The field I crossed was loaded with tank and anti-personnel mines. How I missed stepping on one of them was a miracle. Snipers were the enemy that were left behind by their people, and they would shoot into vehicles passing by at night. The snipers would occasionally hit a truck carrying 55-gallon drums of gasoline, mostly just to harass us. Several times while we were building bridges we would get mortar and rifle fire.

Two months later we moved again to Yonchon, near the Iron Triangle, where I stayed the rest of my time in Korea.

My unit was responsible for building temporary roads, bridges made of rocks, logs, dirt and sometimes pontoons, so the infantry could get their jeeps, trucks, tanks and men to the front. The main roads were about the same as our local county roads without blacktop.

I recall one special job we did on the north bank of the Imjin River. Approximately 120 Chinese with pack mules, jeeps and trucks were hiding in a tunnel about 150 feet long. A P-51 plane dropped a napalm bomb in the tunnel, and everything was burned up. The smell was sickening. We were elected to bulldoze all the bodies and equipment over the side of the cliff so we could use the road. The Stars and Stripes ran the story, verifying the pilot's story with pictures.

My unit also set up the truck tents at Monsan for the truce negotiation teams. Later we made a new pre-fab camp for the negotiation teams at Panmunjom at the request of the Communists/

The truce negotiations started July 10, 1951, and ended July 27, 1953. The fighting continued. In the first five months there were 60,000 UN casualties, of which 22,000 were American.

After a few months in Korea I was promoted to Battalion Motor Sergeant. I was responsible for all equipment and personnel. Many parts needed to repair our trucks were hard to get. However, I found the Chinese truck wheel bearings were the same as ours.

My unit constructed many miles of DMZ — an area separating two enemies. We received mortar and sniper fire at times which was meant only to slow us down. At these times we would call in artillery, and it would stop for a few days. I spent 11 months in combat area and was shipped home. After a short leave at home I was shipped to Fort Dix, N.J., to complete my term.

**********

# CHAPTER 6

# Short Stay at Old Baldy Hill

THE CAPITOL CITY OF SEOUL was in almost total ruins. It was a ghost town with all its burned and blown-up buildings. As we rolled across the Han River on a pontoon bridge built by our engineers, you could see the steel frame remains of the original bridge that had been blown up in the early stages of the war. It was here that hundreds of civilians had died because they were on the bridge when it blew up, all trying to escape the town before the Communists took over. When we cleared the Han River and entered the downtown area of Seoul, the destruction was everywhere. Only a few buildings were still standing, and a lot of the civilian population hadn't as yet returned to the Capitol. I guess they figured they would wait and see if we held it this time around.

The one thing I noticed about all the civilians was the complete look of hopelessness that you could see in their faces. As we drove through the town, you could see old men and women who carried everything they owned on their back. Most of them were poking through the ruins of buildings, probably looking for some kind of food that they could survive on for one more day. Mixed in among the old people were the small children who would run up to all the trucks in the convoy and beg for something to eat. We gave them candy bars or anything else we could give them. What a sad and heartbreaking sight, and it never seemed to end. The whole town looked like a city of the hopeless, and you could see it in their eyes. They would fight over a single candy bar. That's how hungry they were. It was totally unbelievable how much the Korean people suffered during the war. Somehow they would survive. At the moment

*Brothers — Chester, left, and Frank Arnall, near the front in Korea, winter of 1951-52.*

I wondered how they ever could. It was enough to make you cry. I prayed to God that the people of America would never have to go through what these people were going through. Even as I prayed, life in America went on as if nothing was happening in Korea. The only concern that I could detect from the American people was the concern from the mothers, fathers, wives and sweethearts of the young men who were doing the fighting and the dying in Korea.

After awhile we rolled into the countryside and headed north to the frontline. Along by the sides of the road you could see the destruction of trucks and tanks scattered around, a grim reminder of earlier days when a great battle took place here. Most of the small villages we passed were mostly burned to the ground with just a few straw houses still standing. The handful of people here in these small villages stood and stared at us in silence as we passed by. I would bet my last dime that some of these village people were "dyed in the wool" North Korean soldiers who just all of a sudden became citizens of the south, but then, maybe I had been in Korea too long.

One of the amazing sights I saw while in Korea was when we passed through the city of Uijongbu, just to the north of Seoul; the town was completely flattened. Not one building was standing in what once was a fairly big city. What really stood out were all the old rock and brick chimneys that were still standing. They were sticking up into the air all over the town, and what an eerie sight. How in the world could all these chimneys stand up under the bombardment this town had taken? When we passed by the place, it was total silence. Not one person was around. No one on our truck said a word for a mile; then some kid in the Platoon said, "I wonder if they build chimneys like that in the U.S.?"

A little further north we crossed the Hantan River and headed for Yonchon, a city that wasn't far from the frontline and Old Baldy Hill. A little later we passed through the town, and before long we turned off the main road onto what looked more like a cow trail than a road. It led us back into the hills toward the frontline and our destination, which we were fast approaching. Pretty soon you could hear the artillery guns on our side throwing in the big stuff.

It wasn't long until the trucks come to a halt and we knew we had arrived. Just across the road and to the north of us was a group of small hills that was to be our position for the time being. At least until we were needed by the 45th Division. One big hill loomed in the sky past our positions that dwarfed all the others in the area. It didn't take an expert to realize we were looking at Old Baldy Hill. There wasn't a tree or a bush of any kind on top of this hill. We all agreed there wasn't even a sprig of grass left on the top — thus giving it the name of Old Baldy Hill. One of my men remarked that he hadn't seen any hill in all of Korea that wasn't bald.

Once we got into our perimeter defense it was almost dark, and after a while we began to settle in and start the long wait to see if we would be committed into the fight. Apparently the Chinese had kicked the 45th Division off part of the hill, and they were in the process of trying to take it back. You could hear the sounds of battle in the distance, and I for one was hoping the 45th Division would take back what they had lost and then hold it. The fight raged all night, but at daylight we still hadn't been called on to get into the fray.

The next morning the sound of a big fight began again. In my mind I almost knew we would be sent in if things didn't settle down. The firing lasted all night and we still hadn't been called on. I checked around the bunkers and found everybody wide awake. The moment was tense and no one could relax. If called on, we knew this was going to be one hairy operation. None of us had ever been here before, and we didn't have any idea of the lay of the land around the big hill. In a sense we would be going in blindly, and that scared me to death.

On the third night here there seemed to be a reduction in the amount of firing going on. Pretty soon the CO called all the platoon leaders to the Company CP. My stomach was tied in knots. I had the feeling this was the moment we would be briefed and shortly proceed to attack the hill. When I got to the CP, the word was already out that the 45th Division had taken back the part of the hill they had lost and were holding at this time.

A little later we were told that we would be leaving the area the next morning. What a great relief it was to all of us when we realized that for the time being at least, there wouldn't be any combat for us.

The next morning the trucks came back to the road behind us, and we loaded up to leave. We couldn't get out of here fast enough to suit me. Once we hit the main road back towards Yonchon, I breathed a great sigh of relief. It wasn't long until the talk and chatter began to pick up and we began to relax a bit. We had no idea as to where we were going, and it didn't matter as long as we were leaving Old Baldy Hill.

By late evening we pulled into a big valley that was bordered on all sides by high hills and the usual rice paddies. To our great relief we were told we were going into reserve for the first time in months. We took in replacements, and the company began to look normal again. The big tents were set up, and with all the 2nd Battalion it looked like a small city. We would spend over a month here, and I would be getting closer to rotation. But before that happened we would go through a lot of training for the benefit of all the new men. As for me, I would return to the frontline one more time before I would leave Korea.

My last trip to the front would be my most difficult because I knew I was so close to going home. However, I knew that I still had time to put in so I pushed the thoughts of home to the back of my mind. In a few days the man who would take my job would come to "F" Company and I would spend the next two months sort of a "lame duck" (so to speak). I didn't mind that if it meant my days here were getting short. The closer you got to rotation the more the pressure was on you. Days seemed like weeks and weeks seemed like months.

Time dragged on, and before long we were in an intense training program that was meant to keep the veterans sharp and to teach the new men infantry tactics that we used in Korea.

# CHAPTER 7

# Time in Reserve

AFTER EIGHT LONG MONTHS in Korea and most of it spent on the frontline, going into Reserve was almost like going to Heaven to all of us. We lived in a regular tent city that was spread across a big level valley that was the flattest place I saw while in Korea. The whole battalion was set up here, and it wasn't long until it looked like a typical army base. Each platoon in "F" Company had its own sleeping tents and, of course, the kitchen tent was also set up at one side of the company area. The CO and the 1st sergeant had a small tent set up that served as the Company CP. In a few days we all got squared away and ready to begin our stay in Reserve.

One of the first things we did was take a long overdue shower and get a complete set of clean clothes and a new pair of boots. I didn't know how much a man could miss just taking a shower and being clean for a change or getting to shave in clean water instead of the filthy rice paddy water on the frontline. The CO quickly put out the word that he expected everyone to clean up and stay that way while in Reserve. Wouldn't you know it — it wasn't long until some of the guys were bickering about having to clean up a little? As for me, I made a vow I wasn't going to complain about anything. Whatever we had to do would be a lot better than the constant danger on the frontline.

While in this Reserve area, the beer ration was a weekly thing, so most of the troops looked forward to it. Each platoon got a certain number of cases, and each case was broken down and distributed equally to each man in the platoon. Some of us didn't like the taste of beer, so we gave ours to some of the other troops in the platoon.

*Reserve Area — 2nd Battalion in Reserve, early 1952*

One particular night just after the beer had been handed out, I went down to our tent and stretched out on my bunk to get some sleep. Along about midnight I was jolted awake by the blast of what sounded like a 45 pistol. Sure enough — some idiot had gotten to much beer and had shot a couple of holes in the top of the tent next to mine. I couldn't sleep a wink the rest of the night.

The next day nobody knew a thing about it when asked by the 1st sergeant and the CO. The 1st sergeant told us we were all a bunch of liars. He was too big to argue with. Frankly, I thought it was funny after I found out no one got shot. I tried to make a joke out of the whole thing. A little later when I asked the big 1st sergeant if he would have given me the purple heart if I had got hit, he glared at me for a moment and told me to mind my own business. As big as he was, I didn't argue the point.

140

The battalion area was surrounded by a barbwire fence that the CO said was put there to keep out the ever-present civilians who were always around in the hopes of getting something to eat. I wondered if the fence was to keep out the civilians or keep the GI's inside. One of the most pitiful things I saw while in Korea was here at our Reserve area. When all the company had been fed chow, the food that was left over was taken down to the fence and dumped into a hole in the ground to get rid of it. Old men and women, along with small children, would come and eat the food that was thrown away. In other words — what they ate was what we called "slop" at home and was what we fed the hogs on the farm. What a sad and pitiful sight! This went on all the time we were in Reserve. Is there any wonder that I saw many of the GI's give most of their food to some hungry kid instead of eating it himself. As for me, I'm convinced the American GI was the most generous person in the world when it came to feeling sorry for the small children of Korea. You would have had to be there to see how the kids in Korea suffered because of the war. It was so bad it was unbelievable.

**\*\*\*\*\*\*\*\*\*\***

If you doubt my story about the small children of Korea, then read the following story from another Korean veteran:

### Sgt. Donald G. Ringeisen, United States Army

*I was stationed at Camp Gordon, Georgia, in 1953, when I received orders for assignment to Korea. As the years go by, there are certain happenings that bring back the memories of a war area that one seldom hears about. I think that some of these memories that have always stayed with me are those dealing with the sadness of the little children suffering from the atrocities of the leader of a country who wants to take over another country to benefit himself.*

*When I see a little child crying, frightened and lost, my mind goes back to several specific times in Korea.*

*The first occurred when I had left Eighth Army HQ at Seoul where I had been on a detail and was returning to X Corps HQ. On leaving what was left of Seoul, driving along a narrow, well-*

*worn dirt road heading for the old town of Hongchon, I saw movement ahead of me on the right. There were areas where there was quite a lot of snow, and on my right in the distance I could see the Pukhann River. The road had a small rise on the right and then dropped off rapidly into an area where only parts of trees and brush were left from shelling, then a flat area next to the river. As I approached the area, two small children came over the rise from the right. At first I thought there would be some older person with them. They appeared to be about three or so years old. Their little faces were covered with dirt, their noses were running, and their little tummies were bloated from malnutrition. You could tell they had been crying by the tear stains and the dirt on their cheeks. The only thing the little boy and girl were wearing was a little tee-shirt and no shoes. It was very cold and I had on a winter garb.*

*At first I was concerned that there could be a problem, like we had been having with infiltrators throughout this area. After looking all around and seeing no one else, I stopped.*

*The first thought I had was to get them something to eat. I tried to call them over to the jeep. They were so frightened they wouldn't come close. I checked around in the jeep to see what I had that they could eat and found some "C" rations, some candy bars and a couple of cans of malted milk-type drink that I had found on a truck at Eighth Army compound.*

*I took the cans and crawled out of the jeep. As I approached the "little ones," they ran back toward the bank they had come over. They were so frightened that they wouldn't come close. I set the cans down and walked back toward the jeep. They wouldn't take the food. So I went back to the cans and opened each one and took a bite of the "C" ration and candy bars and a drink from the malted milk cans, then went back to the jeep. After cautiously watching me, they walked over to the cans and started to eat and drink. They still wouldn't come near the jeep, so I had to leave them there. As I drove off, my thoughts went back to my beloved wife, who was back home in Kansas awaiting the birth of our first baby.*

*The second occurred a few days later coming in from perimeter patrol. I saw a young Korean boy, who had been staying in a large makeshift cardboard "jib / hut." It was still* very cold and he was wearing a T-shirt, shorts and rubber shoes. We took him back to our area. After getting a medic to make sure his cold wasn't pneumonia, we found an area where he could stay and got him some old "OG's" that he could wear. He was about 10 to 12 years old. His name was Lee. My wife sent clothes and , most important, a "harmonica." A few weeks later, while we were still experiencing some infiltration problems, Lee disappeared. For several days none of us could find him. We thought he had been killed. After several days he showed up with two pairs of little rubber shoes. As he said, "For Sgt. Babysan, and moseamae."

I always wished that my wife and I could have adopted him and brought him to the U.S. He said that his parents left him, his older and little sisters when the North Koreans came through the first time. We all knew that they had been killed. Then the Chinese came through, and his older sister disappeared and his little sister died of starvation.

Soon after we found Lee, part of our unit was alerted for French Indo China. Twenty-five of us were on orders to go as a "forward party" to a place called Dien Ben Phu. It was under siege and fell while part of our unit was on the way to Seoul from where we would fly to Indo China, "Vietnam." Consequently, X Corps was closed out and we were reassigned as a KMAG Unit, and transferred to Wonju.

The third experience occurred while our unit was at Wonju. Early one Sunday morning as I came off duty, I was really tired and walking more or less in my sleep along a road heading down to a mess tent, when I saw a jeep coming over a hill close by with a "ground pounder," waving something in his hand. He was yelling, "Sergeant, Sergeant, your baby is here." The driver was a corporal assigned as our mail clerk. It was a Red Cross telegram, telling me that our baby was here and she and her mother were fine. With tears in my eyes and a big smile on my face, I gave a quick thank-you prayer.

A couple of months later when I received rotation orders, we still couldn't find what happened to Lee's parents. So we still couldn't adopt him and bring him to the U.S. I had heard that a Methodist missionary had just arrived in Wonju. He was going to start a school. I made arrangements for Lee to attend the school.

*My mind still goes back to the day I left the outfit. I can still see Lee crying as I was saying good-bye and biting very hard on a pipe to keep the tears down. I think of how the "little children of this world suffer from the atrocities of their leaders." And we returning soldiers, arriving back home to the "Good Ole USA," with our wives who had gone through "hell" not knowing from one day to the next whether or not her husband was okay, awaiting us with our babies, the future of this world, in her arms.*

*With this in our thoughts, there is only one way to close an episode of memories in one's life like the experiences of Korea. Especially after being blessed by being able to come "HOME" to your wife, daughter and to be blessed with another daughter three years later, and that is by the simple word, "Amen."*

***********

After a few days of getting rested up, the CO informed us we would be starting some training in infantry tactics before long. It's never a good thing to let a military unit loaf around too long. A training schedule was set up sort of like State side. First off, we set up a firing range down the road in the rice paddies. Everybody went through the firing line just like in basic training. You could hear the bitching and complaining for a mile, but it didn't stop the CO from carrying out the training schedule as planned. If the troops didn't complain, you would think something was wrong.

It wasn't long until we switched from the firing range to platoon-sized assaults on the hills in the area. To me this was what the new replacements really needed. We would be supported in these assaults by artillery, mortar and tank fire. This would make it as near to the real thing as possible. Sometimes we would have a few casualties from the close fire support. I guess they figured the more real the training, the better the troops would be on the frontline.

At this point in time, we had a new 1st sergeant who had replaced my old friend Master Sergeant Drummond over on Kimpo Island, and at the same time Captain Vosgien had become company commander. Also, Master Sergeant Frank Arnall was now platoon sergeant of the 3rd Platoon. These were some of the changes that had been made prior to us

144

coming here. A few weeks ago Sergeant Bain, the mess sergeant, had left and Sergeant Jodisen took over his job. Sergeant Ledger, my assistant platoon sergeant, had rotated back to the States on an emergency leave. "F" Company had really undergone a lot of changes.

**********

One day I stood and watched a new group of replacements climb off a truck. They were all young men, and most of them were not over 17 or 18 years old. A few days ago Captain Vosgien had told me that a master sergeant by the name of Robert Larsen was coming to the company and would probably move into the 2nd Platoon. Pretty soon I spotted him and I made it a point to introduce myself to him. Gosh! He was a sharp-looking trooper, and he looked like he wasn't over 18 years old. The thought crossed my mind, "What a shame, in another month or so he would probably look like he was 40, if he lived that long."

After a while we got all the new men settled in, and "F" Company began to get a little more up to strength. However, in all my time here I had never seen the company at full strength due mostly to the fact that we had been up front most of the time. Once we got back to the frontline, I had no doubt the number of people in the company would start getting smaller again.

In a few days my situation in "F Company would change and I would no longer be the platoon sergeant of the 2nd Platoon. I hid my feelings pretty well, but I had a difficult time accepting my new role in the company. From that time on I couldn't wait to get out of Korea.

**********

A few days after the new people arrived, the CO sent for me to come to the Company CP. When I walked in, he told me to sit down that he wanted to talk to me and clear the air about my status in the company. First off, he informed me bluntly that I was no longer platoon sergeant of the 2nd Platoon and that Sergeant Larsen would take over. This should have been good news to me as it probably meant I would be going home before long. The truth of the matter was, it was a shock to me and it showed. He thanked me for the job I had done and, in

145

fact, he did tell me my remaining time here would be short. He told me I would stay in "F" Company until my time was up and that he wanted me just to sort of fade into the background until I left.

That night I sat on my bunk and tried to deal with the new role I had been cast into. Would you believe it — I was deeply hurt because I was no longer platoon sergeant of the 2nd Platoon? I had been with them for so long I had gotten attached to them like family. I was proud of the fact I was one of the 2nd Platoon, and I still considered it "my platoon." Now all that was over and I felt totally alone. With the exception of just a few, most of my old platoon was gone. The "477 - 487" and Little Gibraltar Hill veterans had been wounded, killed or rotated home. I would do just what Captain Vosgien wanted me to do, and that was to be seen and heard as little as possible. It would be a long month and a half before I would leave, and I would return to the frontline one more time before someone would finally realize how long I had been in Korea. I actually worried that they had totally forgotten about me. Truth of the matter was, rifle platoon leaders were hard to find and they made sure I stayed until the last second. Of that, I had no doubt.

✳✳✳✳✳✳✳✳✳

My son was born while we were in Reserve. When I got the telegram from home, it did wonders for my morale. Now I had even more to live, for but at the same time the pressure increased to get out of this place.

The CO rightly guessed I needed something to do, so one day he asked me if I wanted to ride shotgun on a jeep they were sending down to the city of Seoul for some supplies. I quickly agreed, so my trusty M-2 carbine and I mounted the jeep and we headed down the road for Seoul. To me it was a pleasant ride, and I saw some country I had never seen before. The city of Seoul looked the same; however, it looked like more people were here now than before.

It was dark when we got back to the company area. The next morning the CO called me to the CP again and asked me if I wanted to go spend a week with the Greek Battalion down near Seoul and go through a training exercise with them. I took him up on the offer, and it turned out to be one of the most

146

interesting things I ever did while in the army. To me, the Greek Battalion was one of the best units I had ever seen. They treated me like a king. I couldn't believe how quickly and easy they could climb a hill and set up a defense. Frankly, I would have hated to tangle with them. I spent six days running around the hills with them, and I actually hated to leave when my time was up. I shook hands all around and told the company commander what a great unit they had. It was a week I would never forget. I was one tired soldier when I got back to our company area.

For the next two weeks all the companies in the 2nd Battalion would go through the same training the Greeks had gone through. As for me, I was glad when it was all over. Once the company got back to our Reserve area, things sort of began to settle down a little.

**********

The month of May passed, and we were well into June. I kept wondering when my time would come to go home. The weather had turned hot and the rice paddies smelled so bad it was awful. All the more reason I was ready to leave this place; however, my high hopes of leaving would be dashed one more time and it wouldn't be long until it happened.

One day in late June someone came up with a softball, a couple of ball gloves and a bat. We had found a way to pass some time. We found a flat piece of ground behind our tents for a ball field. The game got so serious you would have thought it was the World Series instead of a game being played by a bunch of "dog face" infantry troopers in the middle of Korea. The arguments got so bad no one would umpire, so we finally stopped playing. Next the boxing gloves came out, and before long that was over. Several men were running around with loose teeth and flat noses!

**********

One morning in late June the company commander called everyone to the Company CP for a briefing. I tagged along to see what was going on. The CO told us that we were heading back to the frontline and for everyone to be ready to move out the next day. I started to leave with the others, but he told me to stick around. When we were alone, he told me he hated for

147

me to have to go back to the frontline but no one had said anything about me staying behind. I was deeply disappointed, but I told him I would "suck it up" one more time and hope for the best. Then he told me to find a bunker when I got up front, get in it and stay there and that I wouldn't be called on to go on any patrols. I very much appreciated the fact that he was trying to protect me, but I had been up front more than anyone else in the company, and for some reason I just wasn't worried about it any more. If I died in Korea, I had long ago decided that I couldn't do anything about that. However, at this stage of the game, I felt I would make it out of Korea.

When morning came and everyone was getting ready to leave, it felt strange not to be in charge of the 2nd Platoon. I watched as they all got ready to go. I could see the concern in the faces of the new men and, of course, the combat veterans went about their business just like it was another chapter in their everyday routine they had grown to expect. I wondered what Sergeant Larsen was feeling just now. I hoped that his time in Korea would be easy, but years later I would find out that, that was not the case.

The trucks rolled up and we loaded up. I rode with the CO, and as we headed out I told myself that I hoped this would be my last trip to the frontline. I asked the CO where we were going, and he said it would be just to the northeast of where we were back in the first part of the year. That meant that once again we wouldn't be far from Little Gibraltar Hill. However, this time we would be located near such places as Outpost Kelly, Cavite and Breadloaf Hill. Just past these hills would be 317 Hill. The only difference is that we would be looking at it from a different angle than we did back at Little Gibraltar Hill. I told Captain Vosgien that a lot of the troops in "F" Company should know this area real well and that should be a plus for all the company. He agreed.

When we reached the front it was dark, but a full moon was out. The troops dismounted from the trucks in single file on both sides of the road. We moved out toward the hills that lay ahead in the darkness. Almost immediately I knew where I was. I had been in this area before. I could have walked in blindfolded. I remember one night back in January the 2nd

Platoon had come here on patrol. We had come up this same road and passed through the company perimeter of a unit from the 3rd Battalion. We went down into the valley near Outpost Kelly and Breadloaf all the way to Little Gibraltar Hill. This had been one nerve-wracking patrol, and one of the 2nd Platoon troopers asked me if I remembered. I sure did! We had spent all night looking for a fight with the Chinese. We never did make contact with them.

After the usual confusion "F" Company got into their new position. Just like Captain Vosgien said, I found a home in the bunker of the Como Sergeant. I got squared away for the next and last chapter of my time in Korea to begin. That night about midnight I finally went to sleep with thoughts of my wife and son on my mind and with the screaming sound of artillery shells sailing over us headed somewhere over on 317 Hill.

About two hours before daylight I was jolted awake by mortar fire crashing into the company perimeter. I grabbed my carbine and rushed outside. I would have bet anything an attack was coming. I raced to the top of the ridge and found a place where I could see down to the front of our positions. The 2nd Platoon was just down below me, and I could see people moving around. Apparently the mortar fire had alerted everybody. Lying flat on the ground I waited for something to happen. The mortar fire had stopped, and it was totally still. You could hear a pin drop. I lay on the ground for another 15 minutes, and when nothing else happened I went back down to the Como bunker. I breathed a sigh of relief that no attack had come. Once again the Chinese had let us know that they knew we were here. It was probably their greeting to us on our return to the frontline.

*Left to right: Harold Brokke, Sgt. Marquis, Denzil Batson, Ray Anderson and Sgt. Kubinsky. (Front cover picture)*

## CHAPTER 8

# Back to the Frontline

Out OF PURE HABIT when morning came and after the mortar fire had ceased, I woke up early. After hitting the chow line, I decided to check out the company area and get set in my mind where everybody was located and also check out the terrain to our front. I had been in a lot of different places in Korea for almost a year now. On the frontline I had learned long ago that you didn't take anything for granted. The more you learned about a new position the better. When I got back to my bunker, I already had it all fixed in my mind. I could write a book on the importance of knowing about a new position, especially in a combat zone.

Once again my old 2nd Platoon was located in the middle of the company perimeter with the 3rd Platoon on one side and the 1st Platoon on the other. I went down to the trench line later that day where the 2nd Platoon was located. I borrowed a pair of field glasses from the Como Sergeant and spent the next half-hour checking out Outpost Kelly and another hill called Cavite. It was a desolate looking place. Outpost Kelly had been completely pulverized with artillery and mortar fire, and Cavite wasn't much better. There wasn't enough vegetation on these hills to hide a rabbit. Breadloaf Hill loomed up in the valley below. It didn't take an expert to see why it got its name. I traced the route that I had taken on patrol back in January, and seeing in broad daylight where we had been I wondered how we ever kept from running smack dab into the Chinese. It was for sure I didn't envy anyone going on patrol in this area. As for me, I was convinced this was one of the most Godforsaken places on the Western front.

It wasn't long until patrol action began to be the regular

routine again for "F" Company. Every time someone went out I would sit with my ear glued to the radio or a sound-power phone just to keep up with the action and pass the long nights away. I actually found myself getting the urge to volunteer to take out a patrol. When I mentioned this to the Como Sergeant, he looked at me like I was crazy. After thinking about it for awhile and being so close to going home, I decided I wouldn't try it. However, I never lost the urge to get back into the middle of the fray. Besides, if I had gone to Captain Vosgien and told him what I had in mind, he would probably have had me committed to a "nut-house."

**********

One night my old friend, Sergeant Arnall of the 3rd Platoon, took a patrol out to Outpost Kelly. He only had three other people with him, and all of them were volunteers. The main purpose of the patrol was to find out if anything was happening on Outpost Kelly. I had to laugh when I heard that because Outpost Kelly had been fought over for months and still hadn't been held very long by either side. I had no doubt that Sergeant Arnall would find trouble, and I'm sure he was smart enough to know that, too. It wasn't long until they discovered that the Chinese had an ambush set up on the lower part of the hill. Sergeant Arnall told me later that they were lucky in discovering the ambush before they walked into it. The four troopers circled around the waiting Chinese and came in behind them higher on the hill. When the Chinese realized someone was above and behind them, they scattered like a bunch of quail. One of them was a slow runner, and it cost him his life. The patrol cut him down like a rabbit. Back at the MLR I heard the sudden burst of small arms fire and hoped they were not in a lot of trouble. Later on that night I got the word that they made it back.

The next morning they related to me what had happened. One of the troopers made the remark that we for sure had one less "Chink" to worry about. The dead Chinaman wasn't even carrying a weapon, but he did have a half-dozen hand grenades on him. This happened a lot in Korea. When they attacked, only the ones in front carried weapons. The ones behind carried only grenades. When the ones with the weapons were killed, the others would pick up the weapons and keep coming.

A few nights later with a bright full moon in the sky that lit the area up with an eerie-looking light, the Chinese started a cat-and-mouse game in the rice paddies to our front. It began when they started softly blowing bugles from different places in the rice paddies. Apparently a bunch of them had crawled in close to our company area without being detected. They were good at these kinds of things, so it didn't come as a surprise to me. The company commander was alerted, and the whole company was ready and primed for a fight. One thing that a lot of us noticed real quick was if, in fact, they were going to attack in force, they would have been throwing in the mortar and artillery fire. If they were only out to harass us, they would do exactly what they were now doing in the rice paddies below. That's the way it turned out, but it wasn't over until a couple of our troops spent most of the night in a deadly game of hide and seek with the bugle-blowing Chinese. The "Chinks" finally give it up and faded into the hills across the valley. One of the GI's who had volunteered to go out after them was Raymond Anderson, a Tennessee hillbilly, who had been in my 2nd Platoon for months. When I heard about it, I wasn't surprised that he was one of the volunteers. A couple of weeks later he would lose an arm on Outpost Kelly to a Chinese mortar round. Wouldn't you know it — he would beat me back to the States? I deeply regretted what happened to him.

**********

One morning I walked down to the chow area to eat. I sort of waited until about everyone else had gone because I had written a letter to my wife that I wanted to send back with the cooks to mail. After a while with everyone else out of the area, the cooks finally loaded up and headed down the road away from the MLR. I had been visiting with them, so when they left I was alone in the chow area. Apparently the Chinese were waiting for the truck to start down the road, and they were ready with the mortar. Luckily, I had worn my steel helmet that morning, and when the first round of 120-MM mortar landed and exploded, it blew a hole in the ground big enough to drop a jeep in. It hit so close to me I was dazed for a moment. When I hit the ground, something hit my helmet and it went

153

rolling away from me down the road a few feet. I lay for a moment flat on the ground, and two more rounds came in only further down the road. Apparently they were trying to hit the cook's vehicle, and in the process they came ever so close to ending my career in Korea. I didn't know how close until I went and got my helmet. On one side of it was a jagged crease where a big piece of shrapnel had hit me. Had I not had the steel helmet on, the party would have been over for me. It didn't take me long to hustle back to my bunker after that.

You would have thought the close call I had at the chow area would have kept me close to the bunkers or a hole to get in, but in my case it had happened before, so the very next day I was out and around the company area. I wound up down in the trench line where the 2nd Platoon was located. The trench line was dug about shoulder deep across the front slope of the hill, so when you walked down it only your head was in view. That particular day the sun was out and it was clear as could be. Just before I reached the end of the trench, a bullet snapped just inches in front of my nose. Some sniper had almost killed a platoon sergeant who had gotten careless. When the slug slammed into the dirt bank of the trench, I did a swan dive down to the bottom of the ditch. I didn't move for awhile. The thought crossed my mind, "Is the whole Chinese army after me?" This was the second time in two days they had almost nailed my hide to the wall. I couldn't believe it; no one had said a word about a sniper. I guess I was just there at the wrong time.

There comes a time when a man has had enough. I had reached that point, especially after almost being killed two times the past two days. After 11 months of almost continuous frontline duty with the heavy responsibility of being a rifle platoon sergeant, the constant pressure of being killed at any moment and living like an animal in all kinds of weather, I was a dead-tired and worn-out dog-faced soldier. I had begun to realize I had reached my limit, and I told the CO just that. He said when we left the line that I would probably never return. I hoped he was right. And he was.

When I looked back to last September 1951 when I arrived in Korea, I realized I had survived a year as a rifle platoon leader. All the others I had joined in "F" Company had been gone for months. Only a few men now in "F" Company knew what all I had survived, and they all knew how lucky I was to walk out of Korea alive.

**********

In another week another unit relieved us. When they replaced us, I was more than ready to go. We left the front in bright moonlight just the way we had arrived a few weeks earlier. When we started down the road to where the trucks waited, I followed along at the rear of the column, and for a moment I stopped and looked back. You could see the top of 317 looming in the night sky. This would be the last time I would ever see the frontline. I didn't have any regrets, but this place and its memories would haunt me for the rest of my life.

The next morning we rolled into a little valley somewhere back of the front and found the big tents already set up and waiting. I was worn out and slept like a log that night. From the sound of the snores I think about everyone passed out; at least that's what some kid said who claimed he couldn't sleep because of all the noise.

We hadn't been here two days when the CO called all the platoon sergeants to the CP for a briefing. As usual, I went along to hear what was going on. I couldn't believe it when the CO said they were going back to the same area, only this time they would try to occupy Outpost Kelly in company strength. It got pretty still about then, and you could see the grim look on the faces of all the men. When everyone got up to leave, I was wondering what my status would be this time. Captain Vosgien came over to me and told me bluntly that my time was over and I would stay back and leave for home the next day. They were sending a jeep up from Seoul in the morning to take me back to start processing. It didn't soak in for a moment, and the troops were getting ready to leave, so I hurried down to where the 2nd Platoon was loaded on a truck. It was the hardest thing I ever did. I managed to choke down the emotion and tell them all good-bye. Most of them I would never see again. When they passed from view down the road, I knew it was over for me. I prayed it would end for them soon, but sadly the war in Korea would rage on for almost another year.

I walked back to the tent I would sleep in that night. The

155

*Denzil Batson on the left during basic training at Ft. Riley, Kansas. On the right, Denzil Batson after Korea.*

cooks and supply personnel were still here. The mess sergeant had the coffee going, and I sat down with him to drink some. We talked for awhile, and I finally went back over to the tent. I was finding it hard to believe that Korea was all over for me. As I lay back on my bunk, my mind drifted back to the frontline and I wondered what the company was doing. Over in the hills a short distance away, the big guns were blasting away. I finally went to sleep with my wife and son on my mind. After a year in this hell hole, I couldn't believe I would be seeing them before long.

The next day I rode down to Seoul, and before long I was on board the ship, Marine Phoenix. The ship would take us to Japan and then across the Pacific Ocean to the West Coast of America and then finally home.

The day we started to pull away from the harbor I went up on deck to take a last look at Korea. Over near a small village nestled in the hills I could see an old man with a young boy following him up a path near the rice paddies. Pretty soon they stopped, and both of them gave us a big salute as we sailed away. I hoped that the fighting and the dying we had done would not be in vain, but time would tell. Pretty soon the "land of the morning clam" disappeared into the distance and the war in Korea was over for me.

* * * * *

*Dearest Darling Eva,*

*I left Korea today, and I'm coming home to you. I have lived a whole year for this day, and it's hard to believe that the time has finally come. It goes without saying that I'm thrilled and excited to death that I'll get to be with you before long, and also to see my son for the first time. I'm on board the ship now, and in 14 days we should land on the west coast of America. As happy as I am that I'm coming home, I also feel a deep sadness for the great troops of Company "F" that I left in Korea who are still fighting for their very lives. I will pray for them and hope that some day real soon they will be able to come home to a family such as I am returning to. I will close this now, and I will be seeing you in a few days.*

*All my love,*
*Your soldier husband*

* * * * * * * * * *

Jackson Heights, a godforsaken three-peaked hill that stood a few miles in front of the M.L.R., was the last stand for my old 2nd Platoon as I knew it. I think it only fitting and proper that I write about the last hurrah for them. Jackson Heights stood at the eastern part of the Cherwon Valley and had been fought over for weeks, and neither side had held it for very long. F Company occupied the heights this particular night, and the 2nd Platoon was on the most forward peak. The Chinese started firing a deadly barrage of mortar and artillery fire. At the peak of this attack they blew the bugles and hit the 2nd Platoon in strength. The G.I's fought gallantly, and for a moment they held off the swarming Chinese but lost several men of their own.

A short time later the Chinese hit again and this time they came in greater numbers. Low on ammo, Sergeant Larsen, the platoon sergeant, and just a few others were forced to retreat. Lt. Denmark, who was the platoon leader at this time, ordered the few who were left to get off the hill. He bravely stayed with a wounded man and was captured. About all the platoon was

*Sgt. Molina on the left and Master Sergeant Robert Larsen, who took over the 2nd Platoon when I left Korea. Larsen was one of the few survivors at the battle for Jackson Heights.*

killed or taken prisoner by the Chinese. The rest of "F" company located on the other two peaks of the heights were having their own problems. They were being blasted by a deadly mortar and artillery barrage much the same as the barrage that had hit the 2nd Platoon. A group of 32 Korean civilians carrying supplies up to the hill to the company were completely wiped out. The first sergeant of "F" Company, Master Sergeant Frank Arnall, stood and watched helplessly as the entire group of Koreans was killed by deadly accurate Chinese mortar fire. When it was all over, "F" Company was badly chewed up, especially the 2nd Platoon. They were relieved the next day by another unit. A sad ending for a great group of men whom I was with for months in Korea. For me it was a bitter pill to swallow when I heard about their last battle at Jackson Heights.

# Comments from Some of the Troopers

Following are comments from survivors from the Korean War:

## Master Sergeant Denzil Batson, "F" Company

*In the battle for Little Gibraltar Hill the snow that had fallen made it easier to see. That was a big disadvantage to the Chinese. The troops of "E" Company were finding it easier to spot the Chinese. During one of the lulls in fighting I got up from my prone position on the ground and walked around trying to get warm. My hands and feet were what bothered me the most. Some troops had already got frostbite, and I didn't want that to happen to me. Every chance I got I would repeat my little walk and do some exercises to get the blood pumping again. Then when the firing started again, it was back on the ground until the attack was over. I was determined to make it through this battle. I didn't want to leave the hill until we all left together one way or the other. When morning would finally come, a bunch of us were here to see the end. It came about daylight when the Chinese finally called it quits. We had sustained a lot of casualties in the two days, but we had kicked their rear. They lost a lot of troops as well as losing the hill. I personally know for a fact that a few Chinese I saw wouldn't be around to fight another day.*

## Master Sergeant Denzil Batson, "F" Company

*During our time in Reserve I was sitting in the Company CP one afternoon talking to the 1st sergeant and the company commander about the training schedule for the coming days when a young soldier walked into the CP and asked if anyone knew what platoon Robert McCune was in. He went on to say that McCune was a good friend of his and they had grown up together and were close as brothers. He said he had come over here from his unit to visit him and was excited about seeing him again. Robert McCune was a member of my 2nd Platoon and was killed several weeks before at Little Gibraltar Hill. When I broke the news to him, I might as well have knocked him down. The young soldier was heartbroken. His lower lip began to tremble, and he turned and walked away. He went a short distance, then stopped and came back to where I was, and with a shaky voice he asked me, "Are you sure he was killed?"*

*I had to tell him again that, "Yes, his friend was dead."*

*When he walked away this time, he kept going. You could see the slumped shoulders and the tears flowing freely from his eyes. That night when I lay down on my bunk I couldn't shake the thoughts of the young soldier. For the next month every time I tried to sleep the face of this young man came back to haunt me. I deeply regretted being so blunt when I told him about his friend. I hoped he would come back sometime. If he had, I would have apologized to him for being so blunt. I would never see him again. I didn't even ask him what his name was.*

### Loren Renz, 2nd Platoon

*When the 2nd Platoon took Peak III on Little Gibraltar Hill, I looked around and wondered where everyone was. I didn't realize until later how many people we had lost. Later on in that same day I was wounded.*

### Marvin Bennett, 2nd Platoon

*The mortar attack on "F" Company at the base of Little Gibraltar Hill was the worst mortar attack I had ever been in. When it was over, I had 23 shrapnel wounds. It would be my last day in combat. For a while I thought it would be my last day to live. The pain from the wounds was so bad I passed out.*

### Ken Whitteaker, 2nd Platoon

*I can tell you all about the battle for Little Gibraltar Hill in one word ... awful. The mortar fire was the worst I ever saw. I got hit that day.*

### Richard Uhl, 2nd Platoon

*The day I got wounded on Crete, the mortar round blew me*

*into the air. I was hit in the hand and my leg. When they tried to find my M-1 rifle, it had been blown to pieces. I was lucky I didn't get killed. I would never see combat again.*

### William Ray, 2nd Platoon
*The night we walked headlong into a bunch of Chinese I'm convinced we were so outnumbered by the Chinese it would have been a mistake to start firing on them. The way it turned out they retreated and so did we. Neither side fired a shot. The mistake we made was getting into a minefield. We lost a good soldier when he stepped on a mine.*

### Ron Stewart, 2nd Platoon
*When the Chinese ambushed us on Crete, I had gotten caught on the back slope of the ridge and couldn't get out. The only thing I could do was play dead and hope they didn't discover I was playing "possum." This went on for hours. I finally got my chance to leave. This was after they cut a ring off my finger and took my rifle and cartridge belt. I was lucky to get out alive.*

### Raymond Anderson, 2nd Platoon
*When we were over by Outpost Kelly, I spent a long and nerve-wracking night crawling around in the rice paddies in front of "F" Company's position trying to flush out some Chinese who had slipped in close to our line. They were harassing us by blowing bugles. What made it so bad was I didn't know how many of them there were.*

### Lieutenant Buddin, 2nd Platoon
*When the Chinese ambushed us on Crete, it caught us all by surprise. I jumped into a hole face down. A Chinese hand grenade landed on my back and exploded. I thought it was all over for me. The grenade blew a hole in my back as big as a half-dollar.*

### Oscar Holmes, 2nd Platoon
*One night out on patrol we were about to get hit by the Chinese. The platoon sergeant and I were talking about how we would get down the hill when all of a sudden we realized we*

*were the only ones there. Everybody else had already left, and it didn't take us long to follow suit!*

## William Rice, 2nd Platoon

*One day William Ray and I were sent after a North Korean who had shot a trooper in "F" Company and then fled. We followed him down near a river and he disappeared. I left Ray behind an embankment and told him to cover me while I continued on down by the river to see if I could flush out the North Korean. I walked past a fairly large cedar tree and had gone only a few yards when a rifle opened fire behind me. I whirled around, and the North Korean was lying on the ground dying. He had jumped out behind me, but William Ray had killed him before he killed me.*

## Mike Lester, "E" Company

*When the Chinese overran Peak III on Little Gibraltar Hill, they took some of us prisoners. When they marched us down the hill into the valley, we talked it over among ourselves and decided we were going to jump them and try to get away. We were lucky. We killed all of them and returned to our line. The thought of being in a North Korean prison didn't appeal to any of us. Personally, I would rather they killed me than to be a prisoner.*

## Frank Arnall, 3rd Platoon

*Our company commander, Captain Vosgien, sent three or four of us on patrol over by Outpost Kelly one night. We ran into a bunch of Chinese and chased them away. We killed one of them. Later that night I crawled to the top of Outpost Kelly and stuck a flag in the ground right under their noses. The next day I never did convince Captain Vosgien of what I had done. Apparently the Chinese discovered the flag and removed it.*

## William Drummond, 3rd Platoon

*After we got on top of Little Gibraltar Hill, my big concern was how much ammo did we have. We didn't have enough to stop a counter-attack. I spent a lot of time running around trying to find more ammo for us. If they had hit us hard, we would have been in deep trouble. Luckily, they didn't mount a* major attack until later that evening. By then "E" Company and "G" Company had joined the fight.

### James Twitty, 2nd Platoon

It's a wonder any of us made it out of Korea alive when you think about the battles we were all in. A few times I figured my chances of making it were slim and none.

### George Gunion, Headquarters

Two other guys and I were carrying ammo up to Little Gibraltar Hill when all of a sudden the Chinese threw in some mortar fire. We all three jumped into a hole. A few minutes later I discovered my two friends were both dead. What a shock!

### Stilman Hazeltine, CO "F" Company

I'm convinced if we had waited until daylight to attack Little Gibraltar Hill our casualties would have been a lot worse. I don't think the Chinese thought we would hit back as soon as we did, especially in the dark. We got after them before they had a chance to get more men on top of the hill. Once we got all our firepower on them, they never did recover.

### Robert Larsen, 2nd Platoon

That night on Jackson Heights had to be the worst nightmare I ever went through. Jackson Heights was located quite a ways out in front of the MLR. The 2nd Platoon was the farthest forward of "F" Company. When the Chinese hit, they hit in strength and completely overran our positions. We fired all our ammunition at them, and still they kept coming. I finally called our own artillery in on top of us, they were swarming in so close. They must have thrown a thousand rounds of their own mortar and artillery at us. It finally got to the point where we had to retreat or be killed or captured. The lieutenant ordered us off the hill, and when we told him we wouldn't go without him, he turned a machine gun on us and ordered us to leave. He stayed with a wounded man and fired on the Chinese while a few of us made it down the back slope of the hill. It was a night I would never forget. I never knew what happened to most of the platoon. We had to assume they were killed or captured.

## George Pilkington — "G" Company

*One day I was hauling a bunch of GI's back to O.P. Kelly on my truck. We had to go through an area in the road that the Chinese had zeroed in with mortar and artillery. Pretty soon all hell broke loose and I slid the vehicle to a stop. The mortar fire was coming in thick and heavy, and I jumped from the truck into a ditch and yelled at the others to do the same. Once the mortar fire quite coming, we decided to load back on the truck and keep going. It was nip and tuck the rest of the way. We did finally make it. It's a wonder we didn't all get killed.*

George Pilkington near the front line in Korea. He was later wounded in the battle for Jackson Heights.

George Pilkington was wounded on Jackson Heights, late in his tour in Korea.

## Gordon Gilbert — Heavy Mortar Company

*I was 22 years old when I arrived in Korea, and the first thing that crossed my mind was: "It's tough over here." The first three weeks I was in Korea I had several scrapes with sudden death. They say if you make it through the first three weeks, you might have a chance. What a way for a young man to begin his adult life and, believe me, you become an adult "right now."*

*It was the Kansas line near the 38th Parallel in April 1951 that we were overrun by the enemy. It looked like the only way out was to climb onto the tanks that were attempting to evacuate us. When we tried to climb on the tanks, GI's were being shot and falling off, so we had to find another way out. I found a dry creek bed, and there were three other GI's there. I had the least amount of time in Korea, so I was elected to run down the creek* bed looking for a way out. When I came back for the other GI's, I finally got them to respond to the password, which was a great relief. We did escape and found our way back after walking all night up and down hills and nearly being shot when we finally made it back to our line. We had been listed as M.I.A.'s.

A short time later in 1951 I was first gunner on a 81-MM mortar. Two of our three forward observers had been killed, so I had to go up front and forward observe and call back fire missions. I dreaded to think what could happen to us. Anyway, on the way up to the rifle company's position with my radioman, we decided that they had pulled back to another position and we didn't know it. When we got close to the previous position, we heard this lieutenant behind us yelling at us to "get the hell up here."

At the moment I didn't know what was going on, but when we got up to where the Lieutenant was, he told us we were the luckiest guys in the world. The Lieutenant told us we had almost been stepping on the enemy, and the reason they didn't kill us was if they had fired on us it would have given their position away. It is a miracle that anyone can survive these kinds of situations and make it back home. Let me tell you, when you close your eyes at night, "you just know."

## Bob Pyeatt — U.S. Army

I guess everyone has their story to tell about the war in Korea. Like a lot of other young men, I had been in the Army only a short time when the Korean war started. Just prior to my unit going to Korea, I was involved in an automobile accident that put me in the hospital and killed my closest friend. That meant that my unit deployed to Korea without me. It wasn't long until they were almost wiped out, and to this day I feel a little guilty about not being with them. I'm still alive and enjoy the things this country has to offer, but my friends are gone, killed in Korea.

(Author's note: Bob Pyeatt and I grew up on dairy farms near Halltown, Missouri. We were childhood friends, and little did we realize when we were growing up that the war in Korea would affect both our lives. To this day we are still friends and *stay in touch regularly. One thing is for sure, neither of us will ever forget the war in Korea and the great soldiers who died there.*

*Master Sergeant Denzil Batson and son Denny at Ft. Belveir in Virginia after Korea.*

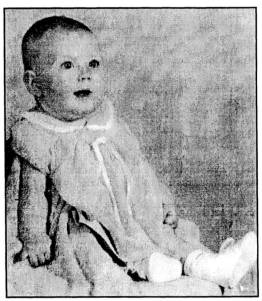

*Five years after my son was born, my daughter, Connie was born.*

# After Korea

THE LAST TEN MONTHS of my time in the Army was spent at Fort Belvoir, Virginia. I was the ranking NCO on a weapons committee that included a 2nd lieutenant and four other NCO's. Our job at Fort Belvoir was to train young recruits who were in basic training on the use of all weapons used by the Infantry. It included the M-1 Rifle, the 30-30 Carbine and the 30 Caliber light machine gun. Also, we conducted classes on the hand grenade and the firing of the 3.5 bazooka. Every recruit who went through basic training at Fort Behvoir fired all these weapons. My main job most of the time was to conduct a nighttime infantry assault with live ammunition. Another one of my jobs was teaching a class on the sniper-scope, which was a night-seeing device that was mounted on a carbine. It had just come out and was used only a short time in Korea. My experience with it under combat conditions wasn't very good. To me, it was too fragile to stand up under rough treatment.

I gave a hundred percent to my job at Fort Belvoir. Some of the young men we trained were sent to Korea, and for that reason I worked hard to try and teach them all I had learned in combat. I hoped that some of the things I tried to teach them would pay off once they got to Korea. I never knew if it did nor not.

Colonel Anderson, my regimental commander at Fort Belvoir, pinned the Bronze Star on me one afternoon at a ceremony held on the parade field at the Fort. As the Colonel read the citation, it mentioned what a great job I had done in Korea. Engraved on the medal were the words "bravery in action." The longer he talked, the more guilty I felt. My mind drifted back to Korea and my old 2nd Platoon that had been destroyed and overrun by the Chinese. Here I stood getting the Bronze Star, and a lot of the troops in my 2nd Platoon were dead and gone. I told myself I didn't deserve any praise for the small job I had done. I wanted the honor to go to the members of the 2nd Platoon. I doubt if any of them got half the recognition they deserved. To this day the Bronze Star medal hangs on the wall in my home. Every time I look at it I think of all the great men who died in Korea. It is a strong reminder to me of just how blessed of God I really am.

During this time at Fort Belvoir, I was fast coming to the end of my three-year enlistment in the army. I had a big decision to make shortly, and it wouldn't be an easy one. When I joined the army three years ago, I had every intention of being a soldier for as long as they would have me. After three years and the war in Korea behind me I wasn't real sure I still wanted to be a soldier. Actually, I liked the military but some things had begun to happen that I didn't like. For instance, I saw troops come to Korea that were so poorly trained it was pathetic. Whose fault was this? In my opinion, it could be laid at the door of the officers and the big Brass. Instead of teaching the troops how to shoot a rifle and do what I called "get down and get dirty," the trend seemed to be to look real sharp at all times and sing a cadence to the troops as they marched double-timed down the street. Some of this was going on at Fort Belvoir, and it burned my rear-end. It's for sure I didn't do any singing to my old 2nd Platoon in Korea. What a joke this crap was, and I resented it with all my being. Discipline among the troops was another thing that I could see lacking. I had been taught at Fort Riley, Kansas, to respect an officer and do what you were told. Now I could see rebellion among the troops at every turn in the road. The reason was because discipline had been replaced to the point where the young men could get away with anything. Too many troops were doing just that, and nothing was ever done about it. There was no doubt in my mind the army was changing, and it had started about the end of the Korean War. It would get worse in the years to come.

One day just before my discharge date they called me in at Regiment and asked me to reenlist in the army. I was told what a great job I had done and that the army needed men like me who had been in combat and were capable of teaching it to the basic trainees. When I asked about several changes that I

*Front row, left to right: Denzil Batson, Marvin Bennett, Raymond Anderson. Back row, left to right, Ron Stewart, Loren Renz, James Twitty, William Rice, William Ray, Richard Uhl, Robert Larsen, Ken Whitteaker, Frank Arnall. Survivors of the Korean War.*

could see happening in the Army and that I couldn't go along with the things that were going on, I was told a good soldier had to "bend with the trend" of the times. My temper flared, but I kept it under control and calmly told them that I had decided in the last five minutes that I wouldn't reenlist. They voiced their regrets, and with that I left the room. Two days later they discharged me at Fort Belvoir on the 15th day of May 1953, at almost the same time the Korean War ended. My career as a soldier was over, and when I was alone that night at home I cried.

After my discharge I moved back to South Missouri with my wife and son. In a few years my daughter, Connie, was born. Later on there would be grandchildren and great-grandchildren.

I never forgot Korea and the awful things we went through. There is no doubt in my mind that America is free today because of what we did in Korea. Every year a few of my old 2nd Platoon members who survived the war get together for a 2nd Platoon reunion. We talk about the war and all the things that

*Eva and I on April 7, 1951,*
*at Ft. Gordon, Georgia*

happened to us. During these times we always remember the ones who didn't make it. As for me, I'll remember all of them until the day I die. It was a pleasure to know every one of them.

\*\*\*\*\*\*\*\*\*\*

Here and now I must say I have left the best for last. It's only fitting that I finish this story and pay tribute to the greatest thing that ever happened to me — my beautiful wife and friend, Eva. In my worst times she is what kept me going. She has been my helper and my pal through all the years after Korea. She has been the greatest mother and grandmother that anybody could want. I don't even come close to deserving her. So all I can say is simply this, "I love you, Eva." You and the kids are what makes it all worth while.

# Conclusion

LOOKING BACK on my year in Korea, it has to be among the most exciting things that ever happened to me. Not only was it exciting, but also nothing in civilian life comes close to the utter terror and horror and sadness of combat. Never before and never again will I have the nerve-wracking responsibility that comes with being the platoon sergeant or leader of an infantry platoon. No other job in the military is as dangerous as the job I held while in Korea, unless it was the men who carried the rifles in my platoon.

The utter hell that comes with combat stays with you for a lifetime. My greatest regret was getting men killed or wounded, and my biggest fear was that I wouldn't be able to get them out once they were killed or wounded.

My hat is off to my 2nd Platoon that I was so proud to be a part of for so long. To me they were the best platoon in Korea. I would be a fool not to think that. I can't remember a time when they were not ready to follow me, every time I asked them. Not one man ever refused to go on a patrol or any other operation we were involved in. I have nothing but the best to say about any of them. To this day I can still hear the groans and cries of the wounded. Some of them I didn't even know their names, but that doesn't make it any less heartbreaking to me.

To the families of the ones who died, I can only say "God bless you" and tell you that your sons are the real heroes of the Korean War. This country is free today because of them, and I will never forget them. At the same time we must know that "freedom is not free." No one knows that any more than the families of the ones who died in Korea.

I would be remiss if I didn't mention the prisoners of war and the awful times they went through. The terror and horror I saw was a drop in the bucket compared to what they went through. Only they know how bad it was in the POW Camps. I salute all of them.

When I got back to America, I got the word one day from a friend who had been with "F" Company that they were fighting for their very lives at a place called "Jackson Heights." A little later I learned my old 2nd Platoon had been overrun by the Chinese and almost destroyed. Sergeant Larsen, who had relieved me and taken over the platoon, made it out with just a few others. So that's how it all ended for my 2nd Platoon and me. Some of us lived and some died in one of the bloodiest wars America ever fought.

— — — — —

Following are the words of a Christmas card that was sent to me by my former company commander, Stilman Hazeltine, just before his death a few years ago. He wrote the lines himself and they touched me deeply.

*I think this is the most beautiful of all,*
*This hour — just at the close of day*
*When I come home and think of you.*

*The sun is setting and the shadows are tall,*
*My thoughts — like a tree — sing and sway*
*As times shared together pass in review.*

*This moment's peace I will recall*
*As I continue on life's wondrous way;*
*Gems of friendship like ours are precious few.*

Sleep well, Stilman, I will never forget you. And I will never forget the great troops of the 2nd Platoon.

The rifleman fights without promise of either reward or relief. Behind every river there's another hill — behind that hill, another river.

After weeks or months in the line, only a wound can offer him the safe comfort of shelter and a bed.

Those who are left to fight fight on, evading death but knowing that with each day of evasion they have exhausted one more chance for survival.

Sooner or later unless victory comes, this case must end on a litter or in the grave.

— *General Omar N. Bradley*